To the Cold Land

33 1/3 Global

33 1/3 Global, a series related to but independent from **33 1/3**, takes the format of the original series of short, music-based books and brings the focus to music throughout the world. With initial volumes focusing on Japanese and Brazilian music, the series will also include volumes on the popular music of Australia/Oceania, Europe, Africa, the Middle East, and more.

33 1/3 Japan

Series Editor: Noriko Manabe

Spanning a range of artists and genres – from the 1970s rock of Happy End to technopop band Yellow Magic Orchestra, the Shibuya-kei of Cornelius, classic anime series *Cowboy Bebop*, J-Pop/EDM hybrid Perfume, and vocaloid star Hatsune Miku – **33 1/3 Japan** is a series devoted to in-depth examination of Japanese popular music of the twentieth and twenty-first centuries.

Published Titles:
Supercell's *Supercell* by Keisuke Yamada
AKB48 by Patrick W. Galbraith and Jason G. Karlin
Yoko Kanno's *Cowboy Bebop Soundtrack* by Rose Bridges
Perfume's *Game* by Patrick St. Michel
Cornelius's *Fantasma* by Martin Roberts
Joe Hisaishi's *My Neighbor Totoro: Soundtrack* by Kunio Hara
Shonen Knife's *Happy Hour* by Brooke McCorkle
Nenes' *Koza Dabasa* by Henry Johnson
Yuming's *The 14th Moon* by Lasse Lehtonen
Toshiko Akiyoshi-Lew Tabackin Big Band's *Kogun* by E. Taylor Atkins

Forthcoming Titles:
Yellow Magic Orchestra's *Yellow Magic Orchestra* by Toshiyuki Ohwada
Kohaku utagassen: The Red and White Song Contest by Shelley Brunt
S.O.B.'s *Don't Be Swindle* by Mahon Murphy and Ran Zwigenberg

33 1/3 Brazil

Series Editor: Jason Stanyek

Covering the genres of samba, tropicália, rock, hip-hop, forró, bossa nova, heavy metal and funk, among others, **33 1/3 Brazil** is a series devoted to in-depth examination of the most important Brazilian albums of the twentieth and twenty-first centuries.

Published Titles:

Caetano Veloso's *A Foreign Sound* by Barbara Browning

Tim Maia's *Tim Maia Racional Vols. 1 &2* by Allen Thayer

João Gilberto and Stan Getz's *Getz/Gilberto* by Brian McCann

Gilberto Gil's *Refazenda* by Marc A. Hertzman

Dona Ivone Lara's *Sorriso Negro* by Mila Burns

Milton Nascimento and Lô Borges's *The Corner Club* by Jonathon Grasse

Racionais MCs' *Sobrevivendo no Inferno* by Derek Pardue

Naná Vasconcelos's *Saudades* by Daniel B. Sharp

Chico Buarque's First *Chico Buarque* by Charles A. Perrone

Forthcoming Titles:

Jorge Ben Jor's *África Brasil* by Frederick J. Moehn

33 1/3 Europe

Series Editor: Fabian Holt

Spanning a range of artists and genres, **33 1/3 Europe** offers engaging accounts of popular and culturally significant albums of Continental Europe and the North Atlantic from the twentieth and twenty-first centuries.

Published Titles:

Darkthrone's *A Blaze in the Northern Sky* by Ross Hagen

Ivo Papazov's *Balkanology* by Carol Silverman

Heiner Müller and Heiner Goebbels's *Wolokolamsker Chaussee* by Philip V. Bohlman

Modeselektor's *Happy Birthday!* by Sean Nye

Mercyful Fate's *Don't Break the Oath* by Henrik Marstal

Bea Playa's *I'll Be Your Plaything* by Anna Szemere and András Rónai

Various Artists' *DJs do Guetto* by Richard Elliott

Czesław Niemen's *Niemen Enigmatic* by Ewa Mazierska and Mariusz Gradowski

Massada's *Astaganaga* by Lutgard Mutsaers

Los Rodriguez's *Sin Documentos* by Fernán del Val and Héctor Fouce

Édith Piaf's *Récital 1961* by David Looseley

Nuovo Canzoniere Italiano's *Bella Ciao* by Jacopo Tomatis

Iannis Xenakis's *Persepolis* by Aram Yardumian

Vopli Vidopliassova's *Tantsi* by Maria Sonevytsky

Amália Rodrigues's *Amália at the Olympia* by Lila Ellen Gray

Ardit Gjebrea's *Projekt Jon* by Nicholas Tochka

Aqua's *Aquarium* by C.C. McKee

Einstürzende Neubauten's *Kollaps* by Melle Jan Kromhout and Jan Nieuwenhuis

J.M.K.E.'s *To the Cold Land* by Brigitta Davidjants

Forthcoming Titles:

Taco Hemingway's *Jarmark* by Kamila Rymajdo

Tripes' *Kefali Gemato Hrisafi* by Dafni Tragaki

Silly's *Februar* by Michael Rauhut

CCCP's *Fedeli Alla Linea's 1964-1985 Affinità-Divergenze Fra Il Compagno Togliatti E Noi Del Conseguimento Della Maggiore Età* by Giacomo Bottà

Sigur Rós' *Ágætis Byrjun* by Tore Størvold

33 1/3 Oceania

Series Editors: Jon Stratton (senior editor) and Jon Dale (specializing in books on albums from Aotearoa/New Zealand)

Spanning a range of artists and genres from Australian Indigenous artists to Maori and Pasifika artists, from Aotearoa/New Zealand noise music to Australian rock, and including music from

Papua and other Pacific islands, **33 1/3 Oceania** offers exciting accounts of albums that illustrate the wide range of music made in the Oceania region.

Published Titles:
John Farnham's *Whispering Jack* by Graeme Turner
The Church's *Starfish* by Chris Gibson
Regurgitator's *Unit* by Lachlan Goold and Lauren Istvandity
Kylie Minogue's *Kylie* by Adrian Renzo and Liz Giuffre
Alastair Riddell's *Space Waltz* by Ian Chapman
Hunters & Collectors's *Human Frailty* by Jon Stratton
The Front Lawn's *Songs from the Front Lawn* by Matthew Bannister
Bic Runga's *Drive* by Henry Johnson
The Dead C's *Clyma est mort* by Darren Jorgensen
Ed Kuepper's *Honey Steel's Gold* by John Encarnacao
Chain's *Toward the Blues* by Peter Beilharz
Hilltop Hoods' *The Calling* by Dianne Rodger
Screamfeeder's *Kitten Licks* by Ben Green and Ian Rogers
Soundtrack from *Saturday Night Fever* by Clinton Walker
The Clean's *Boodle Boodle Boodle* by Geoff Stahl
John Sangster's *Lord of the Rings, Vols. 1-3* by Bruce Johnson
The Avalanches' *Since I Left You* by Charles Fairchild

Forthcoming Titles:
The Triffids' *Born Sandy Devotional* by Christina Ballico
Crowded House's *Together Alone* by Barnaby Smith
5MMM's *Compilation Album of Adelaide Bands 1980* by Collette Snowden
INXS' *Kick* by Ryan Daniel and Lauren Moxey
Sunnyboys' *Sunnyboys* by Stephen Bruel
Eyeliner's *BUY NOW* by Michael Brown
silverchair's *Frogstomp* by Jay Daniel Thompson
TISM's *Machiavelli and the Four Seasons* by Tyler Jenke

The La De Das' *The Happy Prince* by John Tebbutt
Gary Shearston's *Dingo* by Peter Mills
Kate Ceberano's *Brave* by Panizza Allmark
Robert Forster's *Danger in the Past* by Patrick Chapman
Various Artists' *A Truckload of Sky: The Lost Songs of David McComb* by
    Glenn D'Cruz

33 1/3 South Asia
Series Editor: Natalie Sarrazin
From the films of Bollywood and Lollywood, to home-grown *bhangra* hip-hop, Hindu devotional pop and Sufi rock, Sri Lankan rap, Indo jazz and disco, new-wave electronica and diasporic Asian Underground scene, **33 1/3 South Asia** takes readers on a sonically diverse journey through the most significant soundtracks and albums from the twentieth and twenty-first centuries.

Published:
Dil Chahta Hai Soundtrack by Jayson Beaster-Jones
Lata Mangeshkar's *My Favourites, Volume 2* by Anirudha Bhattacharjee
    and Chandrashekhar Rao

Forthcoming:
Coke Studio (Season 14) by Rakae Rehman Jamil and Khadija Muzaffar

To the Cold Land

Brigitta Davidjants

Series Editor: Fabian Holt

BLOOMSBURY ACADEMIC
NEW YORK · LONDON · OXFORD · NEW DELHI · SYDNEY

BLOOMSBURY ACADEMIC
Bloomsbury Publishing Inc, 1385 Broadway, New York, NY 10018, USA
Bloomsbury Publishing Plc, 50 Bedford Square, London, WC1B 3DP, UK
Bloomsbury Publishing Ireland, 29 Earlsfort Terrace, Dublin 2, D02 AY28, Ireland

BLOOMSBURY, BLOOMSBURY ACADEMIC and the Diana logo are trademarks
of Bloomsbury Publishing Plc

First published in the United States of America 2025
Reprinted in 2025 (twice)

Library of Congress Cataloging-in-Publication Data
Names: Davidjants, Brigitta, author.
Title: To the cold land / Brigitta Davidjants.
Other titles: J.M.K.E.'s To the cold land | J.M.K.E.'s To the cold land
Description: [1.] | New York : Bloomsbury Academic, 2025. | Series: 33 1/3 Europe; vol 19 | Includes
bibliographical references and index.
Identifiers: LCCN 2024021979 (print) | LCCN 2024021980 (ebook) |
ISBN 9798765103111 (paperback) | ISBN 9798765103104 (hardback) |
ISBN 9798765103128 (ebook) | ISBN 9798765103135 (pdf)
Subjects: LCSH: J.M.K.E. (Musical group). Külmale maale. | Punk rock
music–Estonia–History and criticism. | Rock music–Estonia–1981-1990–History and criticism.
Classification: LCC ML421.J16 D38 2025 (print) | LCC ML421.J16 (ebook) |
DDC 782.42166092/2–dc23/eng/20240517
LC record available at https://lccn .loc .gov /2024021979
LC ebook record available at https://lccn .loc .gov /2024021980

ISBN: HB: 979-8-7651-0310-4
PB: 979-8-7651-0311-1
ePDF: 979-8-7651-0313-5
eBook: 979-8-7651-0312-8

Typeset by Deanta Global Publishing Services, Chennai, India
Printed and bound in Great Britain

Series: 33 1/3 Europe

For product safety related questions contact productsafety@bloomsbury.com.

To find out more about our authors and books visit www.bloomsbury.com and sign up for our newsletters.

Contents

Track listing

'Külmale maale'
'To the Cold Land'

'Tbilisi tänavad'
'The Streets of Tbilisi'

'Nad ei tea mu nime'
'They Don't Know My Name'

'Meid aitab psühhiaatria'
'Psychiatry Is Helping Us'

'Lõputu laupäev'
'Endless Saturday'

From B-side of the single 'Tere perestroika' (Hello Perestroika)

'Lahendus on kaos'
'The Solution Is Chaos'

From the album *Gringode kultuur* (*Culture of Gringos*) (1993)

'Gringode kultuur'
'Culture of Gringos'

'Tulevik on tunni aja pärast'
'Future Is in an Hour'

The official translation of the album title was 'To the Cold Country'. However, as the title refers not only to a country but also to the metaphorical land, 'To the Cold Land' is used in the translation with the consent of author Villu Tamme.

All the songs except 'Psychiatry Is Helping Us' were written by Villu Tamme, while the author of the aforementioned song is Lembit Krull. The songs also include musical contributions from other band members. Tarvo Hanno Varres, who originally played bass in J.M.K.E., is among those responsible for several notable musical motifs. The album was recorded by Villu Tamme (vocals, guitar), Lembit Krull (bass) and Venno Vanamölder (drums). The album was mixed and engineered by Mikko Karmila and produced by Stupido Twins (Helsinki, Finland).

Acknowledgements

I owe a debt of gratitude to many individuals for their contributions to this book. My biggest thanks go to J.M.K.E.'s frontman, Villu Tamme, and his bandmates for creating such an excellent record, which provided ample material for this book. Additionally, I extend my gratitude to Villu for his deep insights and expertise, which he used to review and refine the manuscript. I am also grateful to Fabian Holt, the editor of the 33 1/3 Europe series, for offering me the opportunity to write the book in the first place and then for wisely guiding me through the process. Furthermore, I am thankful to Indrek Mesikepp and Anu Schaper, who repeatedly provided valuable insights on the historical, musical and the textual aspects of the content, and to Peter Kessler, who initially edited the text linguistically. My sincere thanks to everyone who took the time to speak about the album with me. This research was supported by the Estonian Research Council (grant PSG838).

1 'Jesus Mary, shrieked the hag'[1]
Lyrics, sound and memory

The beginning

In looking back, I realize that for a girl from Tallinn during the regime change at the end of the 1980s, there was nothing surprising about punk. My grandmother lived in the Old Town, which at that time was quite run down and dilapidated but was still a lively part of the city. Instead of today's tourist shops, there were the homes of Old Town residents, and instead of souvenirs, fresh fish, newspapers and other necessities were being sold. Children were playing in the streets, and people were rushing to work or school.

That's why I also saw punks from when I was born. Like the Teddy Boys of the 1950s and the hippies of the 1970s, they loved to be there, despite the Soviet occupation and one-party state which did not tolerate any form of dissent and condemned the degrading influences of Western pop culture. At the turn of the 1970s into the 1980s, deep into the Brezhnev period of stagnation, schoolgirls dressed up as punks with

---

[1] Jeesus Maria, Karjatas Eit – acronym for the name of J.M.K.E. in Estonian from the book *Good Soldier Švejk* by Czech writer Jaroslav Hašek.

clothes from their grandfathers' wardrobes, and to pass the time they pretended to vomit blood while chewing begonias from a flower bush. Less than a decade later, punks were hiding from the militia in the underground passages of the Old Town, under threat of being dragged to the militia station and locked up. Even in the post-Soviet era, when the old restrictions and rules had briefly disappeared and new ones had yet to be introduced, punk was present in Tallinn's Old Town, right in the middle of Town Hall Square. That remained the case until the new century, when police cameras and gentrification gradually pushed punk and other subcultures out of the Old Town to discover new hunting grounds which Tallinn's urban space had to offer. Society had stabilized, business and tourism were flourishing and capitalism had also arrived in the Old Town.

For as long as I have lived I've also known the most legendary Estonian punk band – J.M.K.E. – who gave their first concert in 1986. And it's not just me. Both older and younger generations also know them well. While researching Estonian women in punk, I discovered that *To the Cold Land* (released in 1989; voted Estonia's best music album) and the Sex Pistols' *Never Mind the Bollocks* were the reasons that many discovered punk in the first place. So if you go to a J.M.K.E. concert today, both sixty-year-old and twelve-year-old members of the audience will know the lyrics by heart, regardless of gender identity or social background. Why is that? Songs, when aligned with lyrics, can inspire emotions and embolden people to protest against unjust conditions (Danaher, 2018, 64). This is exactly what J.M.K.E. did, vividly reflecting the times in which Soviet Estonia broke away from perestroika into freedom.

The emergence of punk is often interpreted in the context of the crises which were overrunning multiple countries. For example, at the time of the birth of punk, Britain was able to observe the last bastions of its economy sink (Guerra et al., 2019, 122). The decade in which J.M.K.E. became a cult band in Soviet Estonia was also significant. Estonian punk was a product of the harsh conditions of a totalitarian society in the late 1970s, where there was no room for otherness. With a population of less than 1.5 million, Estonia had been occupied for almost half a century and its people had no hope of liberation. In 1986, however, perestroika was declared as the new political direction, forging the path for a national Estonian awakening in 1988 which itself was followed, even more unexpectedly, by the collapse of the Soviet Union and Estonian independence in 1991. Within this context, punk became the most influential subcultural form of resistance to the regime and, by the end of the decade, temporarily the most popular subculture (Turk, 2013, 79).

What suddenly happened to place punk on such a pedestal in society? Music can easily be seen as a product of a particular time and place (Denisoff and Peterson, 1972, 7–8). *To the Cold Land* is no exception, making the first level of analysis the context of its creation, time and culture. As often with music in conflict situations (Dillane et al., 2020, 1), singing in Estonia provided a way for ordinary people, as well as amateur and professional musicians, to raise their voices in an appeal for justice. These years are remembered as the Singing Revolution, a poetic euphemism for the national mass demonstrations between 1988 and 1991. People came together to sing patriotic songs, whereas only a few years earlier, doing it in public could be punished. It is said that such singing was initiated by punks – a social group which dared to deviate from the Soviet order.

Punk in Western societies represented a repositioning against the existing social structure, accompanied by relevant soundtrack and visual imagery (Colegrave et al., 2002). Punk music became an integral part of the protest, framed by social problems (Danaher, 2018, 68), and a figurative weapon to attack the oppressor (Lieberman, 1989). In Estonia, in the second half of the 1980s, patriotic songs were accompanied by a punk sound, which, in contrast, was deeply ironic, both musically and textually. This makes the second layer for analysing the musical package: the punk sound. The aim of Villu Tamme, writer of most of J.M.K.E.'s songs and the band's guitarist and vocalist, was to create a hardcore punk band, but in his opinion, they failed. Nevertheless, *To the Cold Land* is one of the best hardcore albums of Estonian punk. Stylistically, it is characterized by fast, tight, aggressive and disrupted drums which are backed by equally abrasive bass and, surprisingly, surf rock guitar. The melodies are sometimes laconic and barking but at other times with complex octave jumps, all creating a raw sound.

The third layer is the punk lyrics. Tamme (2001, 463) has defined punk poetry as something badly written: 'Inept, naive, unpoetic. Not at all lyrical. It may contain rhyme, meter, beauty, emotion, inventive imagery, but for God's sake, nothing poetic!' Such a description reveals Tamme's (self-)ironic and quirky humour, which is also present in his song texts. Under the guise of a direct and conversational choice of words, they are often very elaborate. Altogether, with poetry and politics coming together on one album, the album represents with its witty lyrics the end of the Soviet era and the feelings of those turbulent years.

Although J.M.K.E. was far from being the only punk band in Estonia, their songs became the unofficial soundtrack of perestroika and liberation, associated – as often with music in conflicting situations (Piotrowska, 2013, 280) – with opposition, revolt and resistance. Punk lyrics played an important role in bringing Estonian punk into the charts and to masses, even to people who would never otherwise have listened to it. On the one hand, it was a subcultural and literary phenomenon while on the other, it reflected the fears and dissatisfactions of Estonian society in the 1980s (Viires, 2021, 36–7). Their angry music and sharp lyrics vividly reflected the political mindset of the punks of the time and also expressed the discontent of society as a whole.

Thanks to this, Estonian punk musicians could be seen as the first to predict the idea that the life may not continue as it had for almost fifty years in the Estonian SSR. They served as the leading voice of a youth which was rebelling against the Soviet Union. J.M.K.E. and its headman, Villu Tamme, were not only the idols of crazed teenagers, they were also loved by their parents. Songs such as 'Hello Perestroika' were huge hits because their message was relatable to all Estonians, not just kids who wanted to dress up, get drunk and 'rebel' (Kagovere, 2015, 78). In all, the band reflected the contemporary atmosphere, for Estonians this being in their ironic social criticism, what the Dead Kennedys were to some Americans or the Sex Pistols were to the British.

To the Cold Land

The songs on the album were written between 1985 and 1989, with the first being penned a few years before the start of perestroika and the last before Estonia gained independence from the Soviet Union. The album was released when it was finally possible to talk openly about things which could previously only be discussed within the safe confines of one's own home. In addition to directly reflecting the emotions during the end of the Soviet Union, the twelve-song album explores the close history of Soviet Estonia throughout the twentieth century. The track list creates a poetic narrative which leads from Stalinism to perestroika. As the musicians engage in dialogue not only with recent events and the more distant past but also with possible future scenarios, they link past, present and future into an organic whole.

The album also speaks about the collective memory of a generation through the way the performers remembered and sang about historical events which they had not directly experienced. The analysis of the album's music and lyrics illustrates how alternative youth discussed Soviet reality and its power relations. As such, the album resonates with the global punk tradition, where punk lyrics are often part of a larger whole and have a reciprocal relationship not only with their musical environment and visual signifiers but also with the culture that produced them. The collective 'constitutive other' of the songs (Ambrosch, 2017, 101–2), to which punk songwriters made explicit lyrical reference, was the Soviet Union through all its decades, and in the winds of change Estonia was the social context, during the national awakening and perestroika.

Songs such as 'My Grandfather Was a Deserter', 'Beria Is Still Alive' and 'To the Cold Land' delve into the more distant past. They focus on the era of Stalinism, the period between 1940 and 1950 which was marked both by Estonian men fleeing the war and by Stalinist crimes. However, the album is not only a reflection of the past. It also reveals various layers of memory, reflecting as much the youth of the songwriters as it does the events of the immediate period, the 1970s and 1980s. The period up to the mid-1980s is remembered as one of stagnation, marked by the personality cult of the state leader, increasing censorship, and Russification in culture and education, by economic stagnation and a sense of hopelessness in people when thinking that anything could change. The era was also characterized by physical and mental repression of creative people, something which was reflected in songs such as 'Censor' and 'Psychiatry Is Helping Us'.

The six perestroika songs reflect events in real time. The most legendary is 'Hello Perestroika', an expression of people's scepticism about changes under the guise of Soviet optimism. Similarly, 'Hands Up, Virumaa' responds to the movement against phosphorite mining as the ecological threat in Estonia in the 1980s. An explicit stand against the Russification of Estonians is taken in the song 'Internazis', which parodies the mentality of local Soviet-minded people. 'The Streets of Tbilisi' is an act of musical solidarity which condemns the 1989 tragedy in Georgia, the Soviet sister republic in the South Caucasus. There, Soviet troops attacked a peaceful demonstration of Georgian independence supporters using sapper shovels, leaving many dead behind.

The songs can also be categorized ideologically, not only according to historical events. Some are a direct critique of Soviet power, and others are anarchist-pacifist protests. These categories sometimes overlap, with songs being almost always ironic and distantly sardonic. Two other songs reflect the fears which haunted the Soviet people in their dreams and reality – despite an apparent peacetime situation – with these being the anarchist anti-war song, 'They Don't Know My Name', and the pacifist nuclear war theme song, 'Summer of the White Butterfly'.

Song lyrics both 'perform themselves' and are performed. They are always doubly encoded, both as verbal and musical referents. Behind the performance is a real person which thereby makes the vocalist an actor who is playing a role (Ambrosch, 2017, 104–5). Villu Tamme also takes on the most diverse roles in the songs – from internazi to deportee – and sometimes switches between such opposing perspectives during one song. The tone is sharp and deeply ironic, and could not be more direct, as the writer says: 'Basically, the protest by punk bands and some others was expressed as an exaggeration of the ridiculousness of Soviet propaganda. None of the bands here sang "Brezhnev, go fuck yourself" or anything like that' (Rinne, 2008, 131). From a literary standpoint, young musicians move between very different texts, paraphrasing local literary classics such as the Russian tsarist-era Estonian writer Eduard Vilde, and his novel *To a Cold Land* about sending Estonians to Siberia, as well as real-time newspaper reports of events which were taking place elsewhere in the Soviet Union.

The passage of decades has added new layers to the album, and the collective memory through the reception of the album by different generations has come to the fore. Here I am talking about those who didn't live through perestroika, but who made their way through newly independent, capitalist Estonia in the 1990s while listening to J.M.K.E. This was the era in which it was normal for local 'businessmen' to occasionally blow up stalls at night and rob people on the streets in broad daylight. The band also relates to those who were born in the stabilized new century, those who did not experience the chaos of post-Soviet Estonia. In other words, the album tells a story which depends very much upon the listener and speaks to diametrically different groups, from Antifa punks who emerged in the new century to right-wing punks who found their ethos around the end of the 1990s.

Each chapter of this book focuses on a particular period of Soviet Estonian history to which J.M.K.E. refers in song form. Equally important is the analysis of the narratives of those people who were involved: J.M.K.E.'s lead singer, Villu Tamme, bassist Lembit Krull, Finnish music promoter Joose Berglund who released the album, fans from different generations and many others. The album's story also speaks about how pop culture and subcultures were treated in the Soviet Union. There, pop music was more or less censored for fifty years, where opportunities in which subcultures could exist were narrow so that creativity had to be found instead. It offers a historical view of pop culture as society moved from stagnation to perestroika and later from totalitarian society to a liberal economy. It also illustrates how, after moving from a subcultural society to a post-subcultural one, we have moved back to subculture, as seems to be the case with all those J.M.K.E. jackets being worn again by Estonian youths on trams and buses.

2 'I am the censor!'
Bounded subcultures

Prequel: Pop culture under siege

Shortly after Estonia became independent in 1991, my generation found itself in a strange situation in history classes – we had no textbooks. The new republic was in its infancy, and as we had just left totalitarianism, no one had written any. As a result, the lessons went by with a teacher reading out loud the lesson's topics from her papers, and we had to scribble everything down quickly – otherwise, there was nowhere to learn from later. Unfortunately, our history teacher was also blessed with an incredibly monotonous voice, and with the addition of the handwritten material, the lessons were pure torture. I also suspect that we were not too interested in Estonian history, written in rather national romantically at the time. The reason for such an approach was that finally, Estonian historians had the opportunity to write one. But we, the children of the early capitalist generation, were cynical. Families were poor, success was measured by having a neon pencil box, and many of us felt alienated from the nationalist ideals of the previous decade which were so dear to the older generation of Estonians. At the same time, we had heard the stories of the Soviet era for so long that perhaps we somehow stopped capturing the tragedy when Grandma, for example, recalled a relative who had been deported to Siberia in 1949, or died on its way there.

It was only later when I realized how also our generation was influenced by Estonian loss of independence in 1940 after being forcibly annexed by the Soviet Union, even if our memories about the era were more than distant. The fifty-year-long interruption in the development as a free country affected everything, such as our desperate economic situation, the desire for patriotic narratives by the older generation and the relatively low understanding of the need for minority rights, among other things.

The abovementioned disruption happened when Estonia was occupied by Soviet troops in 1940, then by 1941 by German troops until 1944, when it was reconquered by the Soviet Red Army and became part of the Soviet Union until 1991. This centralized authoritarian regime was ruled by the communist party and was characterized by the imposition of a planned economy, a lack of freedom of expression, censorship and, especially in the early years of Soviet rule, abuse of power by the NKVD, the Soviet People's Commissariat for Internal Affairs. Estonian political, social and cultural leaders were murdered or forced into labour camps, or they fled, and, among those who remained, a reign of terror was imposed upon them.

But long-term control of society through terror is not sustainable (Tammela, 2021, 7). Stalin died in 1953, and the period in which Nikita Khrushchev held power was seen as a hopeful thaw (Maripuu, 2015, 94). Compared to the other republics, Soviet Estonia was more privileged as a peripheral region which remained in physical proximity to the West. Thanks to its liberal reputation, the phrase *sovetskii zapad*

('Soviet West' in Russian) followed Estonia and the other Baltic states in other Soviet countries. Literature which could not be printed in Moscow was published here, as the Russian writer, Sergei Dovlatov, who lived in Tallinn in the 1970s, properly illustrates:

> A young Estonian poet published a book with a phallus on the cover. A stylised but recognisable outline. It was impossible to go wrong. . . . I don't want to say it was a special achievement. Just a hallmark of a soft censorship regime.[1] (Dovlatov, 1998, 1172)

Although seemingly more liberal, Estonian culture and music remained under control by the Central Committee of the Communist Party of the Soviet Union. While in the West pop music was seen as a sign of cultural decline after the Second World War, in the Soviet Union an affection for pop was seen as subservience to the West. Pop music, which appeals so much to young people, is often politicized, depending upon and reflecting its social context. The same politicization was enacted by the state authorities, fearing the influence of pop on the ideological palate of the Soviet youth. As a result, pop culture was censored throughout the period, although the degree of censorship varied considerably over the decades.

Despite the powers that be, pop bands and subcultural movements emerged in Estonia, much like they did in the West, assumably already during the late Stalin era of the 1950s to Gorbachev and perestroika in the late 1980s. The totalitarian

---

[1] Translation by the author.

regime saw such people as a threat to the state, even if, in the minds of the country's youth, it was anything but a coup d'état. As a result, there were certain techniques which could be used to control pop culture. Concerts could simply be banned, but for subcultural youths and music fans, other techniques had to be used which remained pretty much the same for half a century: disparagement, criticism and moral and physical pressure.

When searching for examples of the marginalization of subcultural groups which preceded punk, one comes across the earliest groups in the Soviet Union: Teddy Boys (*lõngused*' in Estonian), whose variations were found in many places around the Soviet Union in the 1950s and 1960s. In Tallinn's street scene, the rock-'n'-roll-loving youth stood out due to the way in which they dressed. In the 1950s, this would have meant tight trousers, colourful jackets, brightly striped socks and scarves and thick-soled shoes. In the following decade, thick soles gave way to thin ones, plastic coats, nylon shirts and high-collared jumpers and T-shirts and jeans which were sent by relatives who had fled to the West during the Second World War (Pall, 2004).

Apparently there were not many Teddy Boys in Estonia, and the degree to which they opposed Soviet ideology is questionable (Värv, 2006). However, they received criticism both from the state and from their fellow citizens. Newspapers referred to Teddy Boys as 'one hundred percent hooligans': violators of social order, destroyers of morals, notorious cultivators of the American way of life, victims of the effects of a seething bourgeois culture and germs which had infected the weakest and most backward youths

(*Sirp ja Vasar*, 28 June 1957). But newspapers also reveal the importance of music, often writing about the Teddy Boys' passion for dancing such as how some sixty or seventy young Estonians attended a dance party in Aruküla (a township which is twenty-five kilometres from Tallinn, the capital) because 'Tallinn's dance floors had become narrow and Tallinn's dances were outdated'. As they danced, 'Teddy Boys, profusely sweating, pushed their ladies sharply away from them, then pulled them back by the hand, placed them on their shoulders and on the floor, sometimes in a horizontal position, sometimes turning them completely upside down' (no author, 7 June 1957). Teddy Boys also left their mark on later pop culture. The poems of the most famous Teddy Boy, Arvi Siig, many decades later found their way into the music of the punk band Vennaskond ('Brotherhood' in Estonian).

When compared to their fans, musicians were much easier to control, but attitudes towards bands varied according to style, subculture and decade. In the 1960s, beat music arrived in Estonia and the Soviet Union. Youths behind the Iron Curtain were attracted to Western pop culture, feeling that this socially sensitive music was aimed directly at them. As well as consuming music, they started actively making it, and by the early 1960s guitar bands were springing up all over Estonia. As in the West, beat music became a means of self-expression. According to the musician Vello Salumets (1998, 269), new music allowed them to confront everyday Soviet life, school and their parents, who 'cursed the prevailing order and at the same time tried to force their children into this society'.

Compared to other subcultures, the authorities in this instance developed a more ambivalent attitude towards beat music. On the one hand, the influences of a foreign culture were acknowledged. On the other hand, over time the genre became a weapon of ideological education. Therefore, over the course of several decades, the tone of discussions about 'easy music' – of which beat music was a part – changed significantly from disapproving to rather friendly.

During the Brezhnev era, as the 1960s turned into the 1970s, variations of hippie culture arrived in Estonia. The movement grew into a nationwide systemic subculture, one which was united by slang, meeting places and stylistic elements:

> The emerging phenomenon created a common platform for communication with like-minded people from other Soviet cities, which developed over the decade into a subcultural network or *sistema* (meaning 'system' in Russian). *Sistema* people exchanged information about meeting places, and music events, and swapped addresses and phone numbers of other long-haired pals from other cities. This made it possible to travel – usually by hitchhiking – to unfamiliar cities and to quickly be able to find a place to stay, a meal, and friends. (Toomistu, 2018)

The emergence of local hippies, too, was followed by discussions in the media. A report in the Estonian diaspora newspaper, *Vaba Eesti Sõna* ('Free Estonian Word' in English), for example, painted a picture of Tallinn as a liberal oasis in the middle of the Soviet Union. Even the hippies in Moscow, capital of the USSR, came to Tallinn because life was freer there and the TV showed Finnish television, which had spread across the sea to Tallinn: "'Tallinn is closer to the west. That's why we came here," says a Moscow hippie, leaning against the wall of one of Tallinn's medieval fortresses' (no author, 24 August 1972). Hippies, like punks and fans of beat music, discovered the new trends in pop music through Radio Luxembourg and Finnish television, which was received in Estonia from the 1960s onwards, as well as pirate radio stations such as Radio Nord in Sweden and Radio Caroline and Radio London in Britain. Those stations, operating from ships off the coasts of some countries or in neutral waters, played a lot of rock music, albeit through radio jammers. All of this gave Soviet youths the opportunity to take part in events such as the first Woodstock music festival in 1969 and to listen to The Beatles (Salumets, 1998, 58–64).

While fans could be negatively influenced by social condemnation, more effective official techniques remained available for dissuading bands, such as banning them from performing. The most famous cases date back to the Brezhnev era of the 1970s and the appearance of the first punk bands. One of these was Propeller, formed in 1979 and featuring top progressive rock musicians. Similarly to the schoolboy punk bands, this was seen as a form of musical protest against the Soviet regime's lack of freedom of thought. However, it is difficult to see them as serious punks. Rather it was a project-based band which used punk to provoke the authorities (Ventsel, 2018).

But none of that mattered to the youths. For them Propeller was a punk band. So when riots broke out at a Propeller concert, punks were the first to be blamed. On 2 September 1980, the band was invited to play at the Dünamo stadium (now the Kadriorg stadium) for a football match between teams from Estonian Radio and Estonian Television. Seeing the crowd of fans, the KGB decided to ban the concert as a matter of urgency, fearing that people might riot, and so they did after realizing that their concert had been cancelled. The crowd chanted slogans such as 'Down with Russian power', while cabbages and carrots, which had been brought as prizes for the teams, flew into the air and hit the walls, as musician Allan Vainola recalls (2011, 37–9):

> At some point, people realised that nothing was going to happen and they started walking back through Kadriorg towards the city centre. Feeling increasingly free, the crowd blocked the street from one side to the other. The more agitated members of this crowd started rocking trams and cars which had stopped amidst them, trying to push them over. Out of the windows of the trams could be seen terrified people who had never seen anything like it.[2]

Of course, somebody had to be punished. Radio newscasters were banned from broadcasting, Propeller were approached by the authorities and told they could continue to perform, but without frontman Peeter Volkonski. However, Propeller's music had done its job and, despite the KGB and the militia, new punk bands continued to emerge (Vainola, 2011, 39), followed by scandals. One such band was Turist (Tourist in English). The behaviour of this band and their fans was considered too provocative, and their appearance too rude, while the musicians swore on stage. The last straw was a 1985 concert for school youths at the Sailors Club in Tallinn,

---

[2]Translation by the author.

when some military veterans had gathered on the balconies and they deeply disapproved of what they saw. Over time, however, the strict bans became somewhat formal and even absurd, as evidenced by the fact that the musicians often continued to perform under new names. For example, some of the members of Turist formed a band called Singer Vinger – the suggestion to change the name came from the Ministry of Culture itself, a year after Turist had been banned (Volmer, 8 February 2021).

In addition to direct censorship, the dissemination of information about concerts was controlled. This was made easier by the fact that, in the pre-internet era, such means were more limited. As members of both the Russian and Estonian-speaking rock scenes recall, concert information was spread by telephone, word of mouth and posters. Until the mid-1980s, the posters were mainly put up on school notice boards, and in the second half of the 1980s, it was on the streets which became increasingly widespread as time went on, until the end of the century. Posters were often put up in the dark for fear of the militia. But in the end, there was no protection against them being taken down. The frontman of J.M.K.E., Villu Tamme, remembers a concert which was supposed to take place in the cultural centre of Ellamaa County:

> First I prepared the darkroom, set up an enlarger, mixed the chemicals, chose the right frames from the negatives, made a pile of photographic prints of the faces of the band members, stuck these on some thick paper, added writings in pen and India ink, and splashed on some colour with watercolour. Each poster had a different design, but the photos and

information were the same. Then I gave this roll of posters to Venno [Vanamölder, J.M.K.E.'s drummer at the time], who went around the surrounding villages on his motorbike to put them up. Next, suspicious posters were reported to the militia. The selected militiaman went around the same villages on his motorbike, took down the posters, called the House of Culture, and told them to cancel the concert.

A less restrictive measure to control musicians was known as tarifications, which involved inspections of music collectives. Professional musicians were inspected by a Ministry of Culture commission, most of whom worked for the Soviet Estonian Philharmonic. Amateur music collectives worked for non-musical companies which took responsibility for them, such as cultural houses or state-controlled enterprises along the lines of sovkhozes and kolkhozes. In order to give public concerts, ensembles had to apply for permission from the commission of the Ministry of Culture. They had to declare both the name of the band and the repertoire, although during actual concerts everything was played. During the tarification phase, bands were divided into different categories which determined both fees and venues. While the lowest category allowed an ensemble to perform only in the school or company at which it was based, the highest category allowed them to perform outside of Estonia (Lang, 2020). J.M.K.E. was not exempted from the tarification process because, according to Tamme, there was an actual need for it:

So that there wouldn't be so much trouble. Otherwise all concerts were forbidden. If [the authorities] heard that a punk band was going to play, some guys in leather jackets would turn up and forbid that concert from going ahead. . . On a couple of occasions people had already gathered in the hall and the band went on stage before some men arrived to cancel the whole thing. (Rinne, 2008, 59–60)

In 1986, J.M.K.E. took part in the tarification process to be the only band to fail. Allegedly, the arrangements of the songs did not suit the commission, and the band was disrespectful while singing about eternal flame while wearing hats to cover their Mohawks. Despite the lack of an official permit, the band played anyway. Levels of strictness had changed over time, and the last years of the Soviet Union were much freer than the previous ones had been.

In 1988, J.M.K.E. took part for the last time in the tarification process and easily obtained a permit. Within a few years, the situation had changed completely. The Soviet system was only used as a formality, recalls Tamme: 'Just like in 1986, [composer] Felix Mandre was chairman of the committee but now he had a completely different attitude towards us. We played our songs, he had the lyrics in front of him on paper, and he obviously enjoyed them.' The situation changed drastically over the fifty years, from total bans under Stalin to formal paperwork, which had no impact on reality.

Punk arrives in Tallinn!

Soviet Estonia around the turn of the 1970s and the 1980s was characterized by increasing censorship and Russification. Those years are also remembered for the deaths of the derailed leaders of those policies: Brezhnev in 1982, Andropov fifteen months later in 1984 and Chernenko in 1985. Each of them ruled for a shorter time than their predecessor, so that school children of the time recall that it felt as though they were constantly having a day off school with Tchaikovsky's 'Swan Lake' playing. That's what central television showed when something unexpected happened on a national level, when the actual details of the news couldn't yet be broadcast.

In these circumstances, by utilizing Finnish television, Estonians in the north of the country had their own window onto the free world, through which they could see life flourishing in the supposedly crumbling West. People installed antennas as early as the 1960s so that they could pick up these Finnish channels, especially in the capital, Tallinn. Thanks to this, and in the absence of their own singers and athletes who could compete with Europe, Estonians felt solidarity with their kindred people who spoke a similar language, these being the Finns across the sea (Rinne, 2008, 12).

Of course, watching Finnish TV was forbidden behind the Iron Curtain, and people recall threats of putting signal jammers on the TV towers. At the same time, the media waged an information war, attacking Finland for deliberately building its antennas to undermine Soviet youth by showing them content such as leisure programmes. Apparently, the aim of Finnish television was to dehumanize the Soviet people with programmes about 'western so-called cultural and spiritual values' (no author, 1982, 1). Attitudes towards Estonians were also ambivalent among Finns. There were many who felt sympathy for their neighbours who were enduring occupation, but others were also convinced that their enemies – the communists – now lived on the other side of the Gulf of Finland. Joose Berglund, founder of the Stupido Twins record company which released *To the Cold Land* in 1989, also witnessed this ambivalent relationship:

> A typical Finn knew nothing about Estonia. Estonians were like Russians – the enemy. I was always interested in history, so I knew you spoke a language which was similar to ours. I even had Estonian telly at home. And I remember protests in Finland. We had the ice hockey world championships, and students were holding up placards saying 'Russians out of the Baltics'. Obviously, they got arrested – in Finland! – although they were telling the historical truth. We also had graffiti on my high school wall, probably written by the same students, saying 'Free Estonia!'. It was on the kitchen wall and I passed it every day.

However, relations between the Soviet Union and Finland were not unambiguously negative. In 1964, Finnish president Urho Kekkonen paid a state visit to Estonia. Thanks to this, but even more so because the USSR wanted to earn foreign currency, a ferry service was initiated in the following year between Helsinki and Tallinn, albeit one way: Finns could visit Tallinn, but Estonians could not visit Helsinki. From the beginning of May until the end of September, the ferry ran daily between the two cities, and the number of passengers grew phenomenally. While in 1965 about 9,000 Finns visited Estonia, in the period between 1971 and 1975 around 182,000 Finns went there. This was a record for Soviet countries, and tiny Tallinn had become one of the most popular foreign tourist destinations in the USSR (Pagel, 2015, 290). Viru Hotel, built in 1972 as the first large-scale building designed for foreign tourists, opened another hidden channel for the importation of Western culture into Estonia (Rinne, 2008, 11; Pagel, 2015, 190). The hotel was constructed by Finnish builders according to foreign standards and, until 1980, only guests from capitalist countries were allowed to stay there (Pagel, 2015, 292–3). Finnish musicians also made contact with local ones at the hotel, often performing in the hotel's restaurant, and donating to their Estonian cousins instruments and records (Lang, 2020).

And even if the average Tallinn resident did not hang out at the Viru Hotel, they still had Finnish TV, on which they could see new fashions, soft drink commercials, pop culture and, of course, punk. That landed in Estonia just a few years after it hit the rest of the Western world, in 1977–1978, when Finnish TV showed the Sex Pistols. At the time, Estonia had been part of the Soviet Union for almost forty years. 'It was a shock,' Villu Tamme remembers. 'The best thing that ever happened to music.' These are not just Tamme's memories, but of a whole generation of young Estonians, as visually striking punks, both boys and girls, soon appeared on the cityscape.

Punk has been globally anarchic, nihilistic and deliberately aggressive (Colegrave et al., 2002, 18). A similar rejection of norms was also adopted in Soviet Estonia, by questioning the existing establishment and defying it. Under the conditions of censorship, any expression of anti-state sentiment in official cultural layers was out of the question, and professional Estonian composers were characterized by the escapist creative strategies that allowed them to hide symbolically from power (Kotta). Punk, which also used irony but in a strong, in-your-face way, was suitable for taking a stand. Official opposition to it took place at the whim of the authorities, who tried to make life hell for punks, who were often school kids. All this explains why punk has been referred to as a rebellion by Estonian teenagers against socialist oppression (Ventsel, 2018).

Angela McRobbie (2005, 140) has said that punk was first and foremost cultural. Its self-expression existed at the level of music, graphic design, visual imagery, style and the written word. If demonstrations of the punk mentality in the United States were more musical, the spectrum of manifestations in the UK was broader, gaining ground in fashion, design and aesthetics. One of the most discussed components of the style dimension was clothing, as it was one of the most visible forms which members of subcultures could use to prove themselves (Guerra, 2019, 116). In Estonia, similar to the situation in the UK, the first thing which came into fashion was the punk aesthetic, but this was in its own strange way, because there was a lack of means to make oneself a punk. The demand for products exceeded supply so there was a shortage of various goods, from certain foods to basic necessities. So if the birth of punk fashion in the UK was linked to the Vivienne Westwood shop, in Estonia the punk look was very DIY, caused by socialist poverty. Anything went, whether old violin cases and bath caps, granddad's rubber coat from the First Republic, iron crosses and so on.

The punk appearance made people easy targets for the authorities. In the Soviet Union, there were also legal paragraphs which could be enacted in order to harass punks, such as those which controlled 'parasitism' which could be associated with a lack of work discipline. A parasite was a person who did not work and who lived at the expense of others. Beggars and vagrants had to be caught, and 'antisocial, parasitical elements' had to be punished (Paavle, 2015, 77–9). Similarly, as Villu Tamme recalls, people could be accused of degrading human dignity with their behaviour or appearance under a section of rules which covered improper appearance. Therefore, punks were arrested on the street and taken to the militia, where they were sometimes beaten regardless of gender. These 'visits' to the militia – the first in 1982 and the last in 1987 (Rinne, 2007, 75) – were also recalled by Tamme: 'Usually it was quite simple. You sat in the cell for three hours and all your jewellery was taken away. Your entire jacket could be taken away. If you had a particular hairstyle, they'd cut it off. Sometimes there were beatings, but rarely.' She also remembers open hatred: 'Some employees didn't wear uniforms but sat in the office. If you met them outside working hours, it could end badly. They had a personal mission to destroy [the punks].'

Wearing a punk visage also led to trouble on an everyday level. Similarly, as in Russia and other Soviet Union republics (Pilkington, 2014, 3), fellow citizens on the streets of Soviet Estonia sought to control each other's appearance. School also functioned as an extension of power and as a keeper of order, as the woman from the first punk wave in 1980 recalls:

It was a carnival of who looked the most brainless. In 11th grade, we organized punk Thursdays, meaning we wore punk clothes to school. The girls and I had crew-cuts, we put on our clothes, and to make the effect bigger we agreed to go to the class with about a dozen girls at ten or twenty-second intervals. The first two classes were physics, taught by some man, and the most raucous girl came in last. She was wearing her father's checked Califee-style trousers, which she jokingly called his dad's wedding trousers. In addition there was a green crew-cut, narrow glasses, and a narrow jacket which was split on the back and fastened tightly with safety pins. She was the icing on the cake. After the second lesson, the head teacher ran over and shouted: 'Get yourself in order – you can't come to school like that!' At lunch we met up with that classmate and were just sitting at the dining table, talking and laughing, when someone's sister came to warn us that the head teacher had called all the parents to ask the value of their salaries. Mockingly he asked each of them, 'Don't you have the money to buy a school uniform?' But when it came to the classmate who looked the most fierce, her mother didn't know what she wore to school. She thought that she was wearing corduroys, which were also forbidden – you had to wear a school uniform – and said to the head teacher: 'My God, but she doesn't have any other clothes!' (Davidjants, 2021)

The disturbing visuals were quickly followed by even more disturbing music and punk bands, such as Punk T (formed in 1979) and Generaator M (formed in 1980) which, unlike Propeller's professionals, did not use punk just to make fun. The lyrics, too, quickly became critical of communist society. As such, Estonian punk behind the Iron Curtain differed somewhat from the Western version which inspired it. The Estonian punks of the 1980s had neither a critique of capitalism nor a desire for a left-wing world order. They felt they knew that all too well. They longed rather for a right-wing world order with which they had no direct contact but about which they had created an idealized image with the help of Finnish television, or through magazines sent by relatives from abroad, and so on. On the other hand, such an approach to punk in Soviet Estonia fitted with the socially critical nature of it, simply taking the opposite form of the anti-capitalist punk movement in the West.

Schools were the main venues for punk bands. As mentioned, all bands had to go through a process of tarification, which was basically impossible for a punk band. Performing at school as a seemingly closed event provided an opportunity to circumvent this requirement, so public schools played a crucial role in the birth of punk music. For example, the 10th Secondary School in the suburbs of Tallinn was known as the Tallinn Punk School (Rinne, 2008, 59). Although school concerts were not banned outright, they were still regulated as an extension of the authorities by teachers who feared the same power they represented. As a result, school concerts often ended halfway through, as Hardi Volmer recalls from the Turist concert:

> Other punk bands were completely pushed into going underground, but we were semi-legal so people dared to book us, although sometimes the gigs ended in disaster. A school party could be cancelled after one song because the teachers didn't know what to expect. Or the electricity could be cut off. In 1981–1982, at the construction engineering school, a PE teacher went down into the basement and pulled the electricity for the entire block. He was just so scared. We did nothing special on stage, just talked some dumb gibberish and played music.

Local peculiarities were also directly expressed in J.M.K.E.'s music, which was characterized by a stylistic instability which was common to Soviet Estonian pop as a whole. The dynamic between musical styles which was common in the Western mainstream was absent in Estonia. Information circulated in fragmented form behind the Iron Curtain. It came via foreign magazines, or through pirate radio stations or Finnish TV broadcasts from across the gulf. As a result, local musicians picked up pieces of global phenomena, filling in the information gaps and adapting them to their own environment. As they did not properly imagine how these styles related to each other in their original format, local hybrids of styles and genres tended to emerge. Propeller, for example, synthesized progressive rock and punk in his songs, which could be considered to be mutually exclusive – the former somewhat elitist, the latter born of the working class. The friendly relationship between progressive rock and punk in Estonia in the 1970s and 1980s is also evidenced by the fact that Propeller was named as an influence by many punk musicians, and progressive rock was part of the musical menu of several musicians, including Villu Tamme.

Estonian punk opposed disco and, in its early days, rockabilly. This may seem strange given that post-punk brings the two together, or also when thinking about bands mixing punk with rockabilly, such as those done by The Clash. But in Estonia disco and rockabilly represented mainstream pop. In the 1990s, disco music reflected the sentiments of early capitalist beauty and tough-guy culture, and there was also a significant difference in ideals between rockabilly and punk in the 1980s, as Tamme recalls. The latter was characterized by a desire to make the world a better place whereas, reflecting conversations with rockabilly fans, many of them had very different sentiments, believing that the most important thing was to make a good living for themselves.

All of those general tendencies can also be heard in J.M.K.E.'s music, which is similarly characterized by a knowledge of music which transcends genre boundaries. The band's founders were aware of this from the very beginning:

At every concert we weave about eighty mistakes into our music. . . Our instruments are out of tune, our fingers don't move, the chords are often out of sequence, many lines are sung in Bantu, and those songs that start off with an ultra-fast rhythm slow down after a minute for one and a half times. But actually, our music is also a bit more complex in its harmonies than is conventional punk. Some people don't even consider it punk. In Latvia, for example, a big part of our audience thought it was heavy metal. Certainly [we have musical influences]. The biggest influences are western hardcore bands and the Dead Kennedys, there's even a bit of Alice Cooper and jazz in our songs. (Haug, 1988, 33)

Indeed, the musicians on the album move between different musical traditions. Even though J.M.K.E. wanted to do hardcore, it's difficult to place it within punk. Similarly, Berglund, who released an album in Finland, finds also today challenging to categorize J.M.K.E.:

They're pretty hard to define. There are Dead Kennedys influences and a bit of a surf [rock] sound, but it's definitely not your typical cup of hardcore punk. Not by any means. Also, musically, they are very original. Villu has his way of doing things, a way of playing guitar, one which he learned himself. But maybe that was the reason for their success [in Finland], because they are a unique example of an interesting punk rock band.

Songs about oppression: Censorship and psychiatry

A large chunk of the tracklist on *To the Cold Land* reflects stagnation – the era in which J.M.K.E. became active – which was characterized by an atmosphere of fear and apathy. Tamme recalls: 'There was a kind of indifference, a sense that there was no future anyway. At the time it seemed that the Soviet Union would remain in command forever. Until the end of the 1980s, there was no single sign that we could ever be free. It seemed impossible. [The Soviet Union] was so strong and was determined by destiny.' Like much of the Soviet youth, Tamme cynically believed that everything could have consequences, and that the authorities would use every opportunity at their disposal to put pressure on youth like him:

> One day they'd probably lock me up, so I couldn't plan for the future. I saw no future. I thought about becoming an artist but couldn't get into ERKI [the Estonian National Art Institute]. At that time, the rector, Jaan Vares lived in the lower flat in our building. We weren't close acquaintances, but we knew each other. Then he showed me that letter in his office but, when I started to look at it, he pulled it away and wouldn't let me read it, instead saying simply that 'We are not allowed to let you take the exam'.

It was no wonder then that the 'no future' message resonated so strongly in Soviet youths, just as it did in Britain where young people did not live under a regime of totalitarianism but, from day to day, saw television news reports of ever-rising unemployment statistics and lists of factory closures (Guerra, 2019, 122). In Soviet Estonia, there also existed official ideological restrictions which J.M.K.E. experienced and did not fail to sing about. Thanks to this, songs were born about restraints against freedom of speech and movement – 'Censor' and 'Psychiatry Is Helping Us' – summarizing the experiences of creative people in terms of censorship and controls.

Restrictions on freedom of expression characterized the Soviet Union from the very beginning. Since the Stalin era of the 1940s, the news was replaced by ideologized images. There was no free discussion of social problems and, in the political decision-making process, at best only a final decision was made public, but even then it would be buried in slogans and an avalanche of figures without revealing the path which led to that decision (Tammela, 2021, 11). After Stalin's death the situation improved only slightly. During the Cold War the press became a tool in the propaganda war (Miil, 2013, 107–8). The aim of the media was to disseminate economic, scientific, cultural and political propaganda, as well as to implement communist morals and to combat bourgeois ideology (Kreegipuu, 2015, 166).

In practice, of course, it was impossible to control the media 100 per cent or to exclude dissatisfied voices. Especially in a peripheral country like Estonia, journalists did not submit to the increased censorship and controls of the 1970s and 1980s, or the new level of pressure for Russification, but instead sought out a less ideological and more humane perspective in local newspapers and magazines (Kreegipuu, 2015, 166–7). The closer the time came to perestroika, the freer the media became. Similarly, 'Censor', an echo of the period of stagnation, was inspired by life itself and, in Tamme's words, paradoxically reflected the changing conditions: 'Censorship was everywhere, and then it began to disappear. It was already possible to sing about censorship without there being censorship.' At the same time, the loosening during perestroika did not mean censorship had disappeared uniformly and everywhere. Gorbachev's glasnost – the reduction of secrecy in Soviet society, including the control of the press – only worked to a limited extent. Something could be allowed to be said in one place and forbidden in another (Rinne, 2008, 12).

'Censor'[3] starts with a rapid drumbeat and thickens after only a few dozen seconds to introduce Villu Tamme, a soloist with a distorted, mocking voice, singing mostly in a minor-key harmony:

Hello young poets
Novelists[4], journalists
You've probably got some ideas in your heads
Maybe some opinions, too
You write about what's wrong
About the hushed up truth
We won't accept that
I'm standing in your way
My job is to restrict
My job is to restrain

---

[3] Official translations made mostly by Villu Tamme are used here and below. In some cases, the author of the book has slightly adapted the translations to the original language.
[4] In Estonian, 'novelist' means the author of short prose, but for phonetic reasons, the word is also used in the translation of the song text.

I'm a censor, a censor
I'll turn everything into a beautiful lie
I'm a censor

By singing from the perspective of the censor, Tamme uses the social-critical technique so common in punk, presenting the perspective of the person he is actually criticizing. Wearing the skin of a censor and at the same time being deeply ironic, he turns to the people he represents as a poet and musician who, as social critics, are among the first to feel the weight of repressive power in a totalitarian state. The author continues his monologue:

My taste and the taste of my bosses
Will be the destiny of your works
The many-sided life of our people
I'll show in a pretty and smooth one-sided light
My job is to restrict, my job is to restrain
I'm a censor, turn everything into a beautiful lie
. . .
Because I've got my directives
I'll censor because I've got the power

I can censor you
I've got the power and the orders
I can censor your works
So there won't be anything left but crap

The author aptly and unflinchingly shows what happened to anyone's work when it passes through the apparatus of censorship: everything which could have a critical effect on power, even at the most banal level, was sifted out. As a result, throughout the Soviet era, a whole series of not just propagandist works were published but also some very good authors were left unpublished. Even if one book or another was already in print, it could be banned for seemingly arbitrary reasons and the entire edition destroyed. The fact that censorship was sometimes late to take action shows that the system could not cope with the prospect of total control. For example, in 1971, the censorship board discovered that Arthur Miller's collection of two plays, *After the Fall*, which was supposed to be banned, had been published three months earlier and was already sold out (Kreegipuu, 2015, 195–6).

Another specific control mechanism within the Soviet Union was psychiatry. In essence, this is supposed to be a humane form of treatment which would alleviate suffering. In the USSR, however, it took on the characteristics of a punitive instrument, and specialized psychiatry was widely applied to dissidents and human rights activists. In fact, any dissidence was evaluated from psychiatric criteria. According to the doctrine of totalitarian ideology, the country enjoyed complete economic prosperity, human rights were respected and there were no interethnic tensions. Therefore, the use of psychiatry against dissidents only intensified in the late 1950s because, as Khrushchev argued, only an abnormal or malicious person could be anti-Soviet after the condemnation of Stalin's crimes after his death in 1953 (Hiio, 2021, 237). As a result, many dissidents were recognized as delusional or morbid and, as a method of political punishment, 'anti-Soviet' people were sent to a closed psychiatric hospital. Besides the special camps, the use of psychiatric hospitals was a common form of detention, one with a regime which did not differ much from that of a prison (Kaasik, 2011, 79–88).

In the second half of the 1980s, during the course of perestroika and glasnost, the cases of many wrongly convicted people, including psychiatric abuses, began to be reviewed. J.M.K.E.'s song 'Psychiatry Is Helping Us' also belongs to the discourse, discussing the use of punitive medical practices against dissidents. The song's writer, bass player Lembit Krull, has a distinctly different style from Villu Tamme, both in terms of his harmonic development and rhythmic patterns. The song starts with an actively moving blues bass line and a reggae beat, accelerating quickly into hardcore punk. Soon, progressive rock or jazz elements are introduced, with these being reminiscent of the work of bands such as Nomeansno, an old favourite of Krull. The rhythm changes several times throughout the song, complex bass solos spark a dialogue with the melody, and the harmony changes vigorously, alternating mainly from the minor key. In this soundscape, the writer describes in detail those techniques which were being used to lock up people who talked too much when a less conspicuous solution to a criminal case is what was really required:

> We have now collected all the information about you
> Our man has been following your every step
> We won't prosecute you this time
> Even though you were distributing those leaflets in the street
>
> Sivert Zholdin was freed, Enn Tarto got away too
> But we have a little trick in store for you
> Most of the people may be dissidents
> After all they don't shout it out in the street

But you're mistaken if you think we don't have a medicine to
    prescribe for you
The easiest way is to treat you as a mental case
It also helps us to maintain the reputation of our department

In the first verse, the author speaks of contemporary heroes of the perestroika era, the dissidents Enn Tarto and Sivert Zholdin. Tarto's case vividly illustrates what could easily happen to a dissident in the Soviet Union. One of Estonia's most prominent resistance fighters, he distributed leaflets which proclaimed support for Hungarian and Estonian freedom, just a few years after Stalin's death when a spontaneous uprising in Hungary failed in the face of the pro-Soviet policies of the communist-led Hungarian People's Democratic Republic. A resistance organization which was made up of Estonian school children responded with action in the university town Tartu on the night of 4 November 1956. They were arrested and sent to prison camps.

Tarto was released in 1967, but as he continued participating in resistance activities he was imprisoned again fifteen years later, in 1983 (Made, 2011, 141). The lesser-known Sivert Zholdin was arrested in Tallinn on 2 February 1988, the anniversary of the Tartu Peace Treaty, also for distributing anti-Soviet leaflets. On 14 June of the same year, about a thousand people gathered at the Linda Monument on Harjumäe in Tallinn to commemorate the deportation of Estonians in 1941 – a tragedy that affected many families. Many intellectuals were present to demand the release of political prisoners, including Enn Tarto and Sivert Zholdin, and as a sign of a new freer era those individuals were in fact released (no author, 1988, 1; Suurkask, 2016).

As a separate layer, the song also focuses on what happens behind the closed doors of a psychiatric hospital, revealing how people are drugged and, in the worst cases, driven to suicide. Political psychiatry aimed not only to isolate dissidents from society but also to break their minds or leave the public with the impression that the person was indeed mentally ill. Coercive medical treatment was used to influence people in both cases. Patients could be 'sedated' for regime offences, being put in a straitjacket and/or being isolated, or being given a 'calming' injection. There were also other punishments available at the discretion of the medical staff and guards, such as restrictions on walking and working (or, vice versa, forcing patients to do it); depriving them of being able to correspond with the outside world, or of being able to receive parcels, make appointments or smoke; placing a prohibition on using the library or watching television, and many more. (Kaasik, 2011, 79–89; Noor, 2005, 56–7)

> Psychiatry is helping us
> The dose has been measured out
> You won't be able to think straight
> Psychiatry is helping us, it has never failed
> And no-one will hear of you ever again
>
> We'll have you in a straitjacket, with insulin as the cure
> And soon you'll feel how your brain is getting blurred
> If medication doesn't help, we'll stage a suicide
> Madmen may always kill themselves

In the final stanza, the author takes the narrative to a global context, addressing political institutions which were also familiar to Soviet youths, including Amnesty International, the US Central Intelligence Agency (CIA) and the Chilean military junta which established a dictatorship in Chile in 1973. In this way, the writer demonstrates the powerlessness of the international community in the face of a totalitarian state, notwithstanding whether the intended intervener is democratic or otherwise, but also how one violent regime inspires another.

> Amnesty won't complain, the CIA will respect us
> We'll be an example for the Chilean junta
> The façade of the state is getting cleaner by the day
> While chemicals are destroying your mind
>
> So you're in our grips
> There's no escape
> We advise you to take your life
> We've had enough of your tricks
> Oh no you won't take our advice
> But we have a little trick of our own

Lembit Krull also recalls a personal story behind the song, inspired by the sad life story of a friend of his father. In the early 1970s, he wrote a doctoral thesis in economics, predicting that the Soviet economic system would last until the 1990s: 'As far as I know, he was later sent as a research subject beyond the local psychiatric clinic to Russia. The KGB managed to derail this young man, whose shoulder joints were deformed by injuries sustained during interrogations, and he was socially ostracized.'

The Soviet youths also often voluntarily chose the psychiatric clinic because they feared being drafted into the army: 'I personally went into the madhouse at the time so as not to end up in Afghanistan, although, in 1988, there was no longer so much pressure for that. The doctors helped, and Hasso [Krull – relative and writer], too, who lent me Jüri Saarma's book from which I learned my diagnosis.' During those years the Soviet Union was at war in Afghanistan, and boys were in very real danger of finding themselves in a full-scale war during their two years of military service. This is why feigning schizophrenia or other mental disorders was so widespread, to help youths exempt themselves from military service. Here, the book *Clinical Psychiatry* by the renowned Estonian psychiatrist Jüri Saarma came in handy, with many young men in the 1980s being able to learn the symptoms of schizophrenia so that they could act them out in the military commissariat.

3 *To the cold land*

From war crimes to the fear of disappearance

Escape as a form of protest

Johnny Rotten has reiterated the sentiment of hopelessness which led his generation in the UK towards punk: 'It was a very miserable period. High unemployment. Absolutely hopeless. A furious class war. Literally no future. I wrote my own future. I had to. It was the only way out' (Colegrave et al., 2002, 202). At the same time, the hardcore punk of the 1980s, which had its origins on the West Coast of the United States, was declaring its fierce anti-war stance.

All of this resonated with youths who were growing up in the desperate Soviet reality. By the early 1980s, Estonia had been part of the Soviet Union for forty years. Generations of people had been born and grown up who had never known any other time than under the occupation and for whom the independent Estonia sounded like a distant myth of the past. Compared to the UK, unemployment did not officially exist in the Soviet Union, as it was punishable by law. But there were shortages of everything because the economy was in a terrible state.

The causes of recession lay partially in the Soviet Union's peculiar economic model. The entire economy was industrialized, and private agriculture had been abolished (Laar, 2018, 18). The aim was to synchronize the economic levels of the federated republics, eliminate disparities between them and integrate local economies into the supranational monetary complex. Such a command economy was not based on market prices but on prices which were being set by the state which did not correspond to production costs, demand levels or resource scarcity. As a result, it was impossible to make realistic profit-and-loss calculations, or to identify which industries were consistently making losses. There were also problems with the uneven distribution of raw materials, inputs and labour across the Soviet Union. Economic policy was, too, rigidly expansionist. Large factories were built, employing workers from outside Estonia, and their production was exported outside Estonia (Tannberg, 2005, 375; Rinne, 2008, 12). Fixed food prices, the rise in living standards and the slow growth of agricultural production led to food shortages from the 1970s onwards: rising wages would have allowed more food to be bought, but ideologically fixed prices did not allow supply and demand to be balanced (Kaasik, 2021, 61–2). All in all, people had work, and there could be money, but the shops were increasingly empty.

Second, even worse than economic decline was the new wave of censorship and Russification as the 1970s gave way to the 1980s, which relented in the face of perestroika only in the second half of the latter decade. Russification took place at all levels. For example, a professor of the time recalls the regular compulsory teachers' conferences held under the eloquent title 'Russian as a tool of inter-ethnic communication'. In reality, teachers were learning how to teach Russian while instilling loyalty to the Soviet authorities in school kids. Russian teachers also received higher salaries, and more and more students were enrolled at the university to become Russian-language teachers, which deeply frustrated the local population.

All of this led young people to seek out and adopt a more cynical view of the world than that offered by the communist regime, which could mean both conformity with society and conscious nihilism in some cases. And although Estonian knowledge of punk was somewhat fragmented behind the Iron Curtain, as the decade progressed youths added relevant nuances to it, such as an anarchist world view. By the end of the 1980s, their understanding of punk had become much more comprehensive, and Tamme was considered an expert voice:

People don't know too much [about punk as a phenomenon, so] I will tell you some facts about the punk movement in the west in recent years. A few years ago there was another anarchist congress in Italy, but instead of planning the usual bombings and other terrorist acts there was talk of the increasing threat of war and of laws which were restricting personal freedoms. The point was that punks had taken the initiative at the congress. In one of Finland's better rotaprint punk magazines, Laama, is a rather lengthy article which uses highly rough language to describe anyone who causes undue harm and suffering to animals, such as scientists who carry out animal tests to see how yet another shaving cream or medicine might work on humans. These would be examples of what could be referred to as punk's positive programme. The nihilistic message from most punk bands is also expressed in support of pacifism and environmentalism, and in condemnation of vivisection and social stupidity. On the other hand, an example from last year's German magazine, Tempo included a twenty-page, richly illustrated article which was entitled something along the lines of 'Punk's third generation – the end of a rebellious culture'. The apparent purpose of the lives of these punks was to drink themselves to death. I suppose this is also a form of rebellion against society, but more in the form of surrender. (Haug, 1988, 34)

In this quotation the author's early developed values are clearly visible – involving an anti-war and anarchist world view, intertwined with green political thought. In 2022, the author stated that such a pacifist world view had already formed during his school years:

I've always been an anti-war dude due to my natural intelligence and, somewhere in the early 1980s, I started drawing peace signs and a large letter 'A' [as anarchy] in various places. The peace sign was rarely used at that time but, for example, Eppu Normaali [a Finnish rock band] had a peace sign and 'Peace & Love!' in the Suosikki magazine's patches or shirt advertisements section. That style really suited me.

All those sentiments also found vigorous expression in music, being expressed in songs such as 'My Grandfather Was a Deserter', 'Internazis' and 'Beria Is Still Alive'.

With its strong political subtext, 'My Grandfather Was a Deserter' acts simply as a reflection of such an anarchist-pacifist world view. Like many other small countries, Estonia was caught between two large foreign powers during the Second

World War. Between 1940 and 1941, Estonia was occupied by Soviet troops, and then from 1941 to 1944 by German troops, and finally by the Soviets again in the latter year. Following that process, Estonia lost its statehood for half a century. In the first year of the Soviet occupation alone (1940–1), a significant part of Estonia's political and social elite was imprisoned, deported or executed, and the total loss of life has been estimated at a figure of at least 48,000 people (Sarv et al., 2005, 17). The three-year German occupation led to the extrajudicial execution of many people who contributed to Soviet power. When the Red Army returned to Estonia after the German occupation in 1944, the security organs of the USSR continued to punish the locals from which they had been expelled in 1940. In total, about 90,000 people died due to violent regime in Estonia during the entire Soviet period between 1940 and 1991, which means that with a population of less than 1.5 million, almost everyone lost someone in their family. About the same number of people found the opportunity to leave Estonia during these years; for example, as boat refugees in the 1940s (Rahi-Tamm, 2005, 23–7).

The forced conscription into the armies of both the Germans and the Soviets played an important role in these wartime conflicts, and whether an Estonian man was mobilized into the Soviet or German army could be quite random. An Estonian man who participated in world wars could go through very different military paths depending upon luck and chance and, to some extent, on his own choices. One of the many available options was to leave one's military unit without permission, risking punishment or even jumping off to join the enemy side. There were various reasons for that. Sometimes it would involve a desperate attempt to save one's own life, another time it might be a political stance against the war or, as a third reason, it could simply be a pragmatic choice, one driven by injustice being meted out by one's superiors, or by deficient or insufficient food, or otherwise by bad conditions in the army. For similar reasons, a man could decide not to go to war at all and desert even before a call to the front arrived (Kuldkepp, 2016, 9).

'My Grandfather Was a Deserter' is exactly about such men who decide not to fight and instead choose the supposedly shameful path of desertion. Here, the writer does not place himself in someone else's shoes but instead sings in the first person, one which would be closest to his own position. He criticizes institutional power constructs, including militarism, which glorify heroic narratives. Instead of championing a great idea he prioritizes human life, something which the Soviet regime did not value. The decision not to fight becomes a conscious choice, and the writer later declared that the song was inspired by his pacifist world view. He also rewrites the anti-war concept without the inherent shame which followed it in the Soviet Union that claimed paradoxically to fight for peace. By repeating in every chorus how much he approves of his grandfather's choice, praising him for being 'a real man', he breaks the norms of masculinity which were prevalent in a regime which romanticized the military. But the song can also be seen more abstractly as an individual rejection of claims of power. That word 'deserter' was loaded with great deal of negativity and stigma in the Soviet Estonian media, and was often accompanied by the term 'bandit'. Deserters were spoken of directly and metaphorically, and a deserter could be 'anyone who ran away from a field, factory, or other place of work' (no author, 1943, 1).

The song begins with a deceptively calm beat, only to intensify after the first few words, while being carried by strong guitar riffs, minor-key harmonies and a melodically dynamic bass line. The general minor tonality is disrupted by melodic and harmonic deviations which are characteristic of the entire recording and which break up the simple harmony. For example, the soloist uses an augmented fifth in the melody, giving the piece a slightly eerie sound.

My grandfather didn't go to war
My grandfather was a deserter
He managed to flee to the woods
From his own yard, in the middle of the night

He didn't want to fight
He'd rather live

My grandfather was a deserter – he didn't want to be a
    soldier
My grandfather was a deserter – he was a real man!

The Germans came
Then the Russians
My grandfather didn't go for either
He wasn't interested in their dirty war

He wasn't afraid to die
Just couldn't be bothered to fight

My grandfather was a deserter – he refused to become cannon
    fodder
My grandfather was a deserter – and he's a great example for me

By not taking sides, the author confronts a typical attitude: if you're not with us, you're with them; along with 'the friend of our enemy is also our enemy'. In fact, both Germans and Russians were strangers to Estonians, and it was common for one brother to be mobilized to fight on the side of the Germans while another found himself on the side of the Russians (Kümmel, 2004). As an important aspect, the writer leaves un-ennobled German soldiers, even though they were often remembered in a positive light in Estonia during the Soviet era when being compared to the Russian occupation. In fact, one master was simply replaced by another, and the reality of the Second World War was far more multifaceted. In the 1940s, many people on both sides wished not to take part in the war and also did not welcome the Germans with any great enthusiasm. Here, a popular song expressed the difficult position for Estonians, caught between two strong foreign powers – Germany and Russia – and echoed the feelings of the time: 'Oh shout, people, with all your might, the robber rescued us from the robber's hand' (Laar, 2013, 19–35).

The lyrics can also be interpreted in the form of a memory of the Estonian serf custom of heading into the forest to hide from one's masters, a tactic which was being practised as early as the thirteenth century[1] (Laar, 2013, 13). Although many did just that during the Second World War in the hope of being able to defend their nation's independence, others feared foreign power or simply did not want to fight or later cooperate with

---

[1] Although Estonia had been part of the Russian Empire until 1918, the local elite had for centuries been made up of Baltic Germans – presumably people of German origin who had arrived in Estonia in the thirteenth century.

the Soviets. J.M.K.E. also sing about these people, showing how blurred the lines were. Although the term 'deserter' itself refers to someone who has fled the war, Tamme is obviously singing about a man who went into the woods before he could be enlisted, inspired by the family back-story:

> My own grandfather was not a deserter. In fact he was a bit too old during the war. He had my mother when he was over fifty, and he was in his sixties during the war. He was a schoolteacher and headmaster at that time, in the countryside, while my grandmother was a teacher. Some people say that grandpa didn't care to bother. The Germans came in and he put a statue of Bismarck on the piano. The Russians came in and he put up Lenin or Engels. He didn't want to be on either side.

While interpreting J.M.K.E.'s songs as musical protest, they should contain both disdain for the oppressor and hope for a better future (Dillane, 2018, 15). The former was indeed present in J.M.K.E.'s music but there was no hope, only a deep irony for all sides, a sentiment which expressed the writer's indifference towards a future which was filled with hopelessness. This ironic indifference is also reflected in poetic lines at the end of the song, which allude to the possibility of a third world war and the singer's reaction to the suggestion that a monument should be erected to a deserted grandfather.

> Soon there'll be a third world war
> The end of the whole rotten world
> I'll head for the woods beyond the city
> I'm going to ignore the war
> You can go and wage war

Defend your country
Hope that the neutron radiation
Will catch up with me in the woods

Maybe it will, maybe it won't
If it won't I'll laugh 'ha ha ha …'

My grandfather was a deserter – we should erect a statue for
     him
My grandfather was a deserter – I want to follow him!

Immortal sadists

In contrast to the previous anarchist-pacifist song, 'Beria Is Still Alive' is a frank critique of Soviet power. If not tertiary, the humour is at least secondary, despite unexpected rhymes and puns. In this compelling song, the writer vociferously condemns the crimes of Stalin and Beria. The name of the first of that pair, Stalin, is widely known in history as a Soviet dictator who bloodily united a large part of the world into his empire. Less well known is his right-hand man, the sadistic Lavrenty Beria (1899–1953). For many years, Beria was head of the NKVD, the Soviet Union's powerful People's Commissariat for Internal Affairs (integrated to the Ministry of Internal Affairs in 1946). The NKVD's original purpose was to organize police work and supervise the country's prisons and labour camps. The organization was granted a monopoly on law enforcement in 1934, which lasted so until the end of the Second World War. The NKVD controlled both public order and secret police activities, while carrying out political repression and Stalin-era purges, organizing mass extrajudicial executions of citizens, and developing and running the Gulag system of forced labour camps through which some 15 million people passed under Stalin's authority (Anstett, 2014, 118).

The bloody purges did not pass Estonia by, and the loss of lives during the Second World War and the terror which followed is estimated to have taken out one-fifth of the country's contemporary population. Estonia suffered the most significant losses during the years immediately following its loss of statehood, right up to Stalin's death in 1953 (Laar, 2018, 18). After that things started to change. State leaders realized that it was impossible to continue the old course of violence and that the most essential feature of the Stalinist regime – mass repression – had to be abandoned. In the long term such a policy would have begun to undermine its own foundations. Ironically, the change was initiated by Beria himself. He proposed a sweeping amnesty which would free more than a million defendants, primarily those serving sentences of less than five years. At the time, a total of 2.5 million people of various nationalities were serving their sentences in the Soviet Union's penal labour camps, colonies and prisons (Tannberg, 2004, 37–9).

But the ground beneath Beria's feet was already sinking. After Stalin's death, Beria's own position threatened to become too strong so the ruling elite decided to conspire to get rid of him. Beria was arrested in June 1953 and executed in December of the same year (Tannberg, 2000, 66–7). After Beria's death, the crimes of Stalin and Beria were condemned by the new leader, Nikita Khrushchev. The change in situation was immediately reflected in the local media. While in the 1940s there had been countless Beria speeches and newspaper articles, the picture changed drastically after Stalin's death, with newspapers beginning to report that Beria was an enemy of the people. However, in a situation in which people's rights continued to be curtailed, Estonia remained under occupation, without freedom of speech, public condemnation was not enough to heal the nation's trauma and losses. That was so until information began to circulate during perestroika and a freer atmosphere made it possible to talk about Soviet crimes.

In 'Beria Is Still Alive', the writer does not take on the role of someone else but observes the events with the eyes of a chronicler. Lyrically, the song paraphrases a well-known Estonian children's song about three goslings: 'The snow came down, and the ground turned white, the two little geese can't get out. They are sitting in the barn. What to do, it is winter, and it is bad to walk barefoot in the snow.' These poetry lines resonate with J.M.K.E.'s lyrics: 'The sun rises and lights the country,[2] you can't find out everything from the newspapers; you can't find out who rules the country; you can't find out the name of some death.' So if the song about the goslings is about physical isolation, J.M.K.E. adds the mental aspect to the physical.

> The sun rises and lights the country
> You can't find out everything from the newspapers
> You can't find out who rules the country
> You can't find out what some deaths are called.

---

[2]The lines 'valgeks saab maa' that occur in both the songs mean, in Estonian, that the ground turns white and that the country is lit up.

Beria is still alive
Like dysentery his breath torments the vast country
The bloody dynasty of Beria is still alive
The incurable illness called the KGB

Interestingly, although the writer refers to newspaper censorship in the song's opening words – 'you can't find out everything from the newspapers' – his information came directly from the media, which was gaining increasing freedom during perestroika at the very end of the 1980s: 'I started writing this song when I was reading a newspaper. All sorts of things began to appear about the same time and, when new information came to light, I immediately started writing.' Indeed, if there was little talk of Beria in the intervening decades, in the 1980s one was suddenly able to find plenty of articles which described the brutality which accompanied his rule (Vaksberg, 1988, 3). At the end of the 1980s, national traumas were written about with unprecedented freedom. For example, the newspaper *Saarte Hääl* conducted a history survey in which one could find questions such as 'What do you remember about the deportations in 1949', and 'who were the deporters and how did they behave' and 'how did people feel about the change in state leaders: Stalin's death, Beria's overthrow, Nikita Khrushchev, and later leaders?' (no author, 1989, 3).

Although the song has little direct irony, the wittiness comes from the melodic outline and the lyrical paraphrase which imitates a children's song. As a result, 'Beria Is Still Alive' is itself tonally ambivalent, with overlapping minor and major keys, being reinforced by the cheerful chorus which is sung using the mocking lyrics: 'Beria is still alive, like dysentery his breath torments the vast country.' An imprecisely intoned guitar passage adds to the eeriness by disrupting the song's dominant major. Although the song seems slower than the others, the rhythmic scheme, including the actively moving bass, gives the song a dynamic nature.

The song touches upon violent techniques which were used by the state system to shut down people, having been developed to perfection under Stalin and Beria: 'There lies the body of a political prisoner on a dark country road, the death is called KGB, his eyes are glazed, the man in his straitjacket, his illness is called KGB.' The same sentiment is continued in a repeated refrain: 'Thousands of fighters, dissidents, languishing in prisons, camps. The bloody dynasty of Beria is still alive, the incurable illness called the KGB.' At the same time, the song is not just a reflection of the past, but actively enters into dialogue with the present. By singing that Beria is still alive, even thirty-five years later, the writer expresses a deep belief which is rooted in society. Soviet power is totalitarianism and, despite perestroika, the Soviet Union will never become a free, democratic state.

> There lies the body of a political prisoner on a dark country
> road
> The death is called the KGB
> His eyes glazed, the man in his straitjacket
> His illness is known as the KGB
>
> Thousands of fighters, dissidents
> Languishing in prisons, camps
> The bloody dynasty of Beria is still alive
> The incurable illness called the KGB

The conclusion comes in the penultimate verse, where the author essentially states a thought which is repeated in various songs and in various forms: if you want to ignore power, you have no future in the Soviet Union: 'It's no use thinking in this state, you'll always be considered a dissident'. With these lines, he expresses the global 'no future' slogan of punks, which was an inescapable reality for Soviet youths. He also condemns many of his contemporaries who conformed to the violent and hypocritical system: 'And if you adapt to this society, you'll lose all your humanity', ending his statement with a bold, powerful assessment which equates the crimes of Stalinism with Nazism and racism:

It's no use thinking in this state
You'll always be considered as a dissident
And if you adapt to this society
You'll loose all your humanity

K is for Kolgata and Ku Klux Klan
G is for Gestapo and genocide
B is for barbarism and brutality
B is for Bebebebebebeberiaaa

The fear of disappearance

On an August day in 2022, I went to the local anarchist anti-fascist festival at the Ülase12 social centre in Tallinn. In Estonia, you never know what the weather will be like in the summer. Sometimes it rains for three months in a row, and sometimes the sun shines. This summer, and this particular day, were hot despite the autumn breeze. Even though J.M.K.E. played at two o'clock in the afternoon, the tiny hall was packed to the rafters. By the time the song 'Internazis' started, I had managed to get soaked in beer, fall into the crowd and finally retreat to the back rows, when I suddenly felt a shiver down my spine at the lyrics: 'Who are you to bluster? You're only living on this planet at our mercy. Your thousands cannot fight our millions, and that's why your country belongs to us,' came Villu Tamme's famous lines. A few days ago, former Russian prime minister and interim president, Dmitry Medvedev, responded to Estonian prime minister Kaja Kallas who had called for an end to tourist visas to Russia due to Russia's attack on Ukraine: 'The fact that you are free is not your merit, but our shortcoming' (Laugen, 2022). At that moment, it dawned on me how strikingly similar today's Russian rhetoric about the war in Ukraine is with that of the Soviets, which many of my peers and parents still vividly remember.

The same rhetoric is paraphrased by 'Internazis'. On one side it mirrors the rejection of the pro-Soviet authorities and citizens in favour of the democratic sentiments of the Estonian people during perestroika while, on the other side, it expresses the deep, fully justified Estonian fear of Russification. Until the end of the First World War, the Estonian population was rather homogeneous. Estonians were peasants in the Russian Empire and had not mixed well with any of their foreign conquerors who had ruled here since the Middle Ages: Germans, Swedes, Danes and Russians. The population reached the 1 million mark around 1900. By 1915, it had risen to around 1.2 million. In 1934, Estonians made up about 88 per cent of Estonia's population, Russians about 8 per cent, followed by Germans and Swedes (Kaasik, 2021, 49–50).

This remained the case until about 1945. Then, as a result of occupation, the composition of the population began to change. By 1989, when *To the Cold Land* was released and Estonia's independence was only two years away from being restored, the proportion of Estonians in the population had dropped to around 60 per cent: Estonians were in danger of becoming a minority in their own country. This was not a natural migration but a deliberate line of activity by the communist party within the Soviet Union. The purpose was to reduce differences between populations in the peripheral regions of the USSR, to develop an advanced socialist society and to create a new social group: the Soviet nation in which the national cultural aspect would be of little importance. The ultimate aim was to suppress national identity to such an extent that, sooner or later, the indigenous peoples of the federal republics would be 'swallowed up' (Kaasik, 2021, 49–55).

Here, a practical means was migration. People from other federal republics were sent to Estonia to work and were often supported with housing which was not provided to the local population (Kaasik, 2021, 49–55). As a result, entire regions were becoming Russian-speaking, such as the Lasnamäe district of Tallinn and the entire north-eastern part of Estonia, in Ida-Virumaa. The language and cultural policy of the USSR did not encourage immigrants to learn the local language as the language of administration was Russian, so there were Russian schools, and various other Russian-language services (Kaasik, 2021, 81–7).

As time went by, Estonians who feared extinction in their own country started to make efforts to limit immigration. In 1980, the sailing regatta was held in Tallinn as part of the 1980 Moscow Olympics, for which extensive Olympic facilities had to be built which brought even more labour into Estonia. By then, Estonians already knew what to expect from such immigration. The problems were multifaceted: medical care deteriorated even further, there were not enough kindergarten places, and even less housing was available (Kaasik, 2021, 70–1). People also expressed their dissatisfaction publicly, and there were youth riots of 1980, along with civil disobedience, struggles between youth groups of different ethnicity, and the spread of politically incorrect jokes.

The fear of Russification was also discussed in a public letter by Estonian intellectuals, the so-called Letter of Forty, 28 October 1980 with the official title 'Public Letter from the Estonian SSR'. The authors stated: 'We wish Estonia to become and remain a country where no one feels insulted or hindered because of their mother tongue or origin. A country where there is understanding and no hatred between ethnic groups, a country where cultural unity in diversity prevails, and no one feels threatened by their national feelings or culture.'[3] The letter was signed by forty intellectuals who wanted to protect against the actions of the Soviet authorities both the Estonian language during Russification and also those schoolchildren who had gone out onto the streets a few weeks earlier in mass protests. The letter was sent to main local newspapers but

---

[3] Author's translation

none of them dared to publish it, but this did not stop a copy of the letter circulating among the people (Kiin et al., 1990).

As the decade progressed, the pro-Estonian independence movement grew even more. One such was the Popular Front, which was initiated on 13 April 1988 by the later prime minister of the Estonian SSR, Edgar Savisaar. It was a legal pro-Estonian opposition that supported perestroika and became extremely popular (Põlluste, 2019, 7–9). Not only did ethnic Estonians join the Popular Front, but the independence of Estonians was also supported by various ethnic minorities who felt connected to the fate of Estonians, such as the country's Armenian population (Davidjants, 2016, 132).

The remarkable resonance of the Popular Front and the political activation of local pro-Estonians had a frightening effect on Soviet-minded people. This, in turn, created favourable conditions for establishing the International Movement in 1988 which supported the unity of the Soviet Union. The movement, although leaving the impression of being a citizens' initiative, was in fact born as a result of strings being pulled by the Moscow party elite. Intermovement held the meeting on 12 July. A secretly organized public rally was attended by Russian-speaking workers who were living in factory dormitories in Tallinn. On the eve of the event, leaflets were left in residential buildings, and workers from the fishing company *Eesti Kalatööstus*, Dvigatel and other companies in Tallinn were invited to the rally via radio (Põlluste, 2019, 8–17).

All of these sentiments which were escalating at the end of the 1980s were also reflected in the song 'Internazis'. The word in this title carries a complex political meaning. In the late 1980s it was being used to refer to an activist of the International

Movement. The song lyrics are written from the point of view of such an internazi: a Russian-speaker who despises Estonians, something which is emphasized by Russian-language phrases in the refrain. At the same time, it reflects upon pro-Nazi ideology which seeks to cancel the right of existence of people who are of other ethnic backgrounds, and believes in the superiority of its own culture, showing how similar communism and Nazism really were from the point of view of the ordinary person.

'Internazis' is characterized by a minor key, where the tight beat and the arrangement disrupt melody. The aggressive singing style resonates both with belligerent internazis and, through a caricature performance, reflects the lyricist's own attitudes towards the antiheroes of Estonian independence. Similarly, the writer dwells on the topic of ecological threat of phosphorite mining and the green movement during perestroika (discussed in the following chapter), which expressed Estonian national resentment at the waste of Estonia's natural resources.

Do you know what colour is democracy?
It's not blue, black or white[4]
We need proper food, phosphorite
It can only be had under the red flag

Who are you to bluster?
You're only living on this planet of our mercy
Your thousands cannot fight our millions
And that's why your country belongs to us

---

[4]Colours of Estonian flag

One of Intermovement's arguments was that 'we used to live in a friendly way'. Indeed, many immigrants who did not know Estonian lived in their own bubble. They were probably unaware of their privileges vis-à-vis the local population, even in terms of the question of basic housing. That was so until the locals began to assert their rights more vocally under the changed conditions. A survey which was conducted in 1986 showed that only 10 per cent of Russians saw the existence of tensions in interethnic relations, while for Estonians the figure was 58 per cent. Within a few years the situation had changed drastically. In 1989, a total of 75 per cent of respondents among Russian-speaking schoolchildren perceived interethnic tensions (Põlluste, 2019, 5–10).

The rhetoric of the Intermovement quickly became aggressive and provocative, as can be seen from the Interfront leaflets: 'We are the masters here. We fought for this country . . . They think that Estonia is only for Estonians. But have we done a little work so that Estonians can drive cars, and have their own houses and cottages?' The leaflet ends with a call for 'bloody pogroms' (Põlluste, 2019, 15). A similar style of speech is imitated in J.M.K.E.'s song. The author has squeezed into a few lines of poetry the contempt shown by foreign powers for Estonian national symbols and important landmarks by trivializing those national symbols such as the barn swallow, and the colours of the Estonian flag. Villu sings with bravado: 'Soon your tribe will be wiped from the face of the earth,' and these words resonate directly with the tiny nation's ultimate fear:

Ah, you don't fancy the Soviet regime
Soon your tribe will be wiped from the face of the earth

We'll turn the barn swallows into barn sausage for Moscow
Wash it down with milk from a blue-black-white carton

Your country will be tied to ours forever
You know what colour is democracy?
Our flag is red and so is the blood
Running from your noses unless you fuck off!

The culmination of the Intermovement was on 15 May 1990, when their rally near the parliament building on Lossiplats in Tallinn grew into an attack on Toompea Castle, location of the government offices. The attack was motivated by the change in the country's name and the adoption of the symbols of the Republic of Estonia. Gorbachev had, on 14 May 1990 – just a day before – decried as null and void these decisions which had been taken by Estonia's Supreme Council. A day later, Intermovement activists gathered among 3,000 Russian-speaking workers from large factories in Toompea, who eventually broke into the courtyard of the castle. They demanded the immediate reintroduction of the Estonian SSR and the USSR symbols and the abandonment of the aim of restoring the republic. At 6.45 pm, prime minister Edgar Savisaar responded by means of a radio broadcast in which he called on the Estonian people to defend the government building in Toompea with the famous words:

The supreme council and the Government of the Republic of Estonia call on the people to defend the government building on Toompea. The gangs of Interfront and the United Labour Collective Council have surrounded Toompea Palace and are attacking it. I repeat, Toompea is under attack. There is a coup d'état – an attempted coup d'état – taking place in Tallinn and in parallel in Riga to overthrow the legitimately-elected government. We call on the Popular Front, we call on the Union of Labour Collectives, we call on the Citizens Committees, on all the innovative forces on Toompea. I repeat: the Supreme Council of the Estonian Government and the parliament of the Estonian Government call on the people to defend Government House on Toompea. We are under attack! (Savisaar, 1990)

People heard the appeal and came in their masses, forcing the protesters to leave. On 25 August 1990 any activity by Intermovement was banned (Laar et al, 2018, 136–7).

To emphasize the polarization and opposition between 'us' and 'them' and to mock the lexicon of Soviet-minded people, the chorus is almost fully sung in Russian. As Villu Tamme recalls, the Russian phrase 'Ah, you don't fancy the Soviet regime?' was common when a Russian-speaking person started to scold an Estonian wherever that may be, for example, on the street: 'Especially if that Estonian happened to be a punk or was otherwise "non-Soviet". This scolding was an entirely everyday phenomenon, which in some cases ended in beatings and in others in the loss of personal possession while in many cases you could get away with simply being scared.'

Why are you hanging around here? (I'm an internazi!)
Bloody Estonian (I'm an internazi!)
Want to be beaten up? (I'm an internazi!)
Maybe you don't like the Soviet regime?
Nahui! [Fuck off! in Russian]

4 'They don't know my name'
Pacifistically about anarchism

The butterfly and the atomic bomb

I have often thought that every generation has its own fear. My parents, born in the 1950s in the wake of the Second World War, were afraid of war while already for those born in the 1960s, the memory of war seemed like a distant past. My own generation, born during the 1970–1980s, feared AIDS, which linked sexuality – a rather suppressed topic after the Soviet past – with death. My own students today share a deep concern about climate change, and – again – the war.

What did the young people, born around the 1960–1970s, fear in the 1980s? A nuclear bomb, which many of them still see in their nightmares. Each of these fears has found a reflection in pop culture. The fear went so deep into our bones that many of us still feel frightened by the sound of fighter planes, or unexpected loud sounds. 'When fighters flew over our roof, I always sprinted into the room and turned on the radio,' recalls a friend, born in 1971. 'And when I heard *Vikerviisid* [a popular music programme], I knew – no need to worry, everything's OK.'

'Summer of the White Butterfly' is exactly such a story about the atomic bomb. Of all the anarchist-pacifist songs on the album, it is among the most symbolic. It is not a direct criticism of the Soviet Union, and yet the song was deemed unsuitable for power. Following the Stalinism, culture demanded life-affirming positivity and optimism, with there being great conquests to be made, from land to space and, to paraphrase Stalin's speech at the time of the bloody repressions in the 1940s, life was getting better and happier even if reality said the exact opposite. 'Summer of the White Butterfly', on the other hand, was somewhat a distorted image of the demands of optimism. Instead, it reflected the paranoid atmosphere and fears of the Cold War, accentuated by eerie music which was combined with overly cheerful lyrics.

In the middle of the 1930s, in the wake of political changes in Europe, an international arms race began, in which the USSR also participated. With violence, Stalin had created an area of heavy industry and, according to various estimates, the USSR's peacetime defence spending amounted to 15 per cent of its total economic output. The Soviet Union remained on heightened military alert for more than half a century (Mertelsmann, 2015, 145). An essential part of the arms race was the nuclear programmes being run by both the United States and the Soviet Union. After the destruction of the Japanese cities of Hiroshima and Nagasaki by American atomic weapons in August 1945, both countries continued to build more and bigger bombs (Swift, 2009).

The arms race led many Soviet and American people to fear that nuclear war could happen at any time. Both governments urged citizens to prepare to survive an atomic bomb, and during school drills many generations of Soviet youths practised putting on gas masks (and, in poor times, marlin masks). Throughout this period, there were also a great many articles in the Soviet Estonian media which expressed that fear. It was also mixed with the belief which was being propagated by the government that the nuclear threat came only from the West, while the Soviet Union fought fiercely for world peace. In 1958, for example, the newspaper of the small Estonian island of Hiiumaa proclaimed on its front page that the threat of atomic death was being confronted by the united will of the nations. People worldwide were joining in furious protests to put pressure on their governments through mass actions as they followed the noble peace initiative of the Soviet Union (no author, 1958, 1). Over subsequent decades media coverage of the atomic bomb grew even greater. Soviet Estonian citizens read about the US soldier who tried to kill himself by detonating a nuclear bomb (no author, 1963, 4). Similarly, kids were frightened by articles about the nuclear threat even in children's magazines. An issue of children's and youth magazine *Säde*, for example, contained an instructive story about how the Americans had managed to lose an atomic bomb in the Mediterranean, which is why people no longer dare to eat or drink for fear of nuclear poisoning (Käär, 1966, 3). Such coverage continued for several decades until the end of the Soviet era.

At the same time as the authorities were whipping up fears of a possible nuclear catastrophe, ordinary citizens were left in the dark about their own country's foreign political messages, recalls Villu Tamme:

We didn't know what the Americans were doing, but part of the Soviet propaganda was that the US wanted to start a nuclear war right away, and we had to protect ourselves. We were constantly afraid that it was going to start, and we had to be prepared because they were the aggressors. In America, they were afraid of exactly the opposite – of Russian nuclear bombs, although there was little talk of that.

Despite the lack of information, news did circulate, and from unlikely sources. The views of the other side may not have come from newspapers but from fiction: 'I remember one of Stanislav Lem's Ijon Tichy stories, how he found himself on a planet with people whose language seemed familiar. There were the planets, Rasha, Chayna, and Merka, and people feared the god called Abom. It was from this Cold War satire, written by a Pole, that I learned what hysteria actually existed in America.'

J.M.K.E.'s 'Summer of the White Butterfly' begins with a short polyphonic intro in which the bass and guitar engage in a rhythmic dialogue. The harmony balances between minor and major, only being clearly major in the chorus. The harmony of the verse, with its dense drum beat, suggests a minor key, but there are elements of major in the vocals – leaving the listener with the feeling that their expectations have been disrupted, and creating a musically ambivalent soundscape. Structurally, the song comprises several formal units, avoiding the classic verse-chorus form but adding different motifs and instrumental interludes.

Considering authenticity as a cultural construct rather than an inherent quality of an artist or music, pop culture can be seen as an endless series of quotations and paraphrases, being always somehow addicted to its past (Reynolds, 2011). Songs indirectly enter into dialogue and comment upon each other, and production and consumption are symbiotic (Traube, 1996). Similarly, 'Summer of the White Butterfly' can be seen in an abstract dialogue with songs which allude to nuclear fear, or use the nuclear bomb as a metaphor for power, such as the Stranglers' 'Nuclear Device', the Sex Pistols' 'God Save the Queen' or the Dead Kennedys' 'Kill the Poor'. The latter, one of Tamme's own favourites, does not directly discuss the threat of nuclear war but rather does so through a satiric prism of class issues and the division of the people, as if the more privileged class could survive a nuclear catastrophe. Textually, Tamme is similarly satirical, taking the symbolism even further, and using the metaphor of the white butterfly to talk about nuclear disaster. According to Estonian folklore, seeing the first butterfly in spring, a white one, means a difficult summer, while a yellow one means a happy summer. By referring to the nuclear cloud, which is also often depicted as white, the author bridges the gap between archaic wisdom and the dangers of modern times.

I always knew ever since my childhood
I wouldn't see the white butterfly in the spring
That meant a sad summer
Summer and sorrow hand in hand
Oh I didn't want to believe it

In the beginning of that summer
Only white butterflies were swarming
They were everywhere

Though I didn't believe them, I foresaw evil
My heart foresaw sorrow, my heart foresaw death

The summer came, hot and in full bloom
It was sunny and people were happy
Voices on radio talked of tension but we didn't listen to them
Didn't want to hear the thunder of aeroplanes

We hadn't seen death
We hadn't seen ruins
Life had been good to us
Now, in the middle of the summer
We saw all we hadn't seen before

It's the summer of the white butterfly
The blaze of a thousand suns
This summer won't leave any memories
All dissolves, even sorrow and joy

The summer came bleeding
Death raining from the sky, death exuding from the sea
The earth was lifeless
Guarded only by vultures and white butterflies

The summer was cruel, the summer was hot
The world was full of colourful suns
Radios fell silent, no listeners left
No need to listen, you could see it yourself

We saw death, we saw ruins
Life was still good to us
At the end of the summer, life was still good to us

The song does not explicitly refer to a nuclear catastrophe. However, such a meaning is captured in the image 'blaze of a thousand suns', a paraphrase of the book *Brighter Than a Thousand Suns* by Austrian author Robert Jungk, who studied the making and dropping of the atomic bomb from the point of view of the nuclear scientists. Tamme, then, continues to sing about nuclear winter but somewhat unexpectedly, the song is not overtly horrific or depressing. Instead, the writer drifts over a dark subject with a sense of humour. He promises that after a thousand years of nuclear winter, which also alludes to the biblical millennial kingdom of peace, there will be a summer of colourful butterflies which, according to Estonian folklore, symbolize an eventful summer in which anything can happen:

> The summer of white butterfly is over
> It's time for the winter of a thousand years
> We endured the summer, we'll endure the winter
> The winter full of colourful butterflies

By singing about nuclear winter, he introduces a scientific concept which was widespread in the 1980s, both in the Soviet Union and in the United States. In this process, fires follow a nuclear disaster, and dust will be sent into the stratosphere, blocking out the sun. All of this leads to a global cooling of the climate, resulting in frost and famine across the planet, and leading to mass population deaths (Goure, 1985, 7). The Soviet media also painted a grim picture of the consequences of nuclear war:

> The nuclear winter will see total darkness for at least the first month, and by the eighth month around fifty percent of

normal light levels will have returned. When the dust cloud finally disperses, the composition of the air will be so ruined that ultraviolet rays will begin to reach the Earth in quantities many times greater than are safe to endure. (Palu, 1985, 2)

While Tamme does not freeze on the frightening image, the discussion of nuclear disaster does not remain superficial either. Beneath the humour, the writer's deep irony boils. The optimism is illusory and teasing, underscored by the chanting vocal style. It is clear that no one can survive a nuclear disaster, and a nuclear winter is a dead winter. The song, therefore, comes across not as naive and moralizing but as a paraphrasing of Soviet forced optimism, a mockery of it:

> The summer of the white butterfly is over
> It's the beginning of a new world
> We endured the summer, we'll endure the winter
> While we wait for a brand new spring

Back in the summer of 2022, Tamme said that 'Summer of the White Butterfly' was one of the last nuclear fear songs he wrote. Later, everything became buried under perestroika, and the topic lost its relevancy. But a year after the interview, when some time had passed since Russia had attacked Ukraine and Vladimir Putin was more frequently using the threat of a nuclear attack, he reinterpreted his words: 'I see now that the topic has become to the point again due to Russia's constant nuclear threats. Before that there was a degree of bliss to be enjoyed in thinking that this topic was completely lost to history.'

Militancy in the sheepskin of pacifism

An essential theme in Estonian punk – pacifism – is linked to the lingering fear of war both in Afghanistan, to which conscripted young men were being sent, and to the aforementioned nuclear threat. Following the successful atomic bomb tests in 1949 and the discovery of its new-found strength, the Soviet Union changed its rhetoric, putting the struggle for peace in the centre of its propaganda. But although the Soviet Union preached peace, this struggle was paradoxically militant, and the constant talks about peace accompanied the arms race. Peace campaigns were an important platform from which a new, early Cold War vision of the world was communicated to the population of the USSR, and it was also a central feature of Soviet foreign policy. Newspapers increasingly referred to the power of the USSR and the strength of the global peace movement as a guarantee of the international stability, in contrast to hostile capitalist powers, which Soviet strength would provide for all. The language of peace through force also allowed the USSR to reverse its anti-nuclear stance, declaring the Soviet acquisition of the bomb as a 'victory for the cause of peace'. All in all, peace became shorthand for the USSR's muscular and moral patronage of the world's oppressed peoples, even if it was an empty rhetorical exercise (Johnston, 2008, 259–66).

In this robust military pacifism, ordinary people couldn't express their thoughts freely, making ambivalent their relationship to the rhetoric of peace. They could support peace simply because their families had suffered at the hands of state violence, perhaps in the form of deportation during the Stalin regime. But the endless words from the authorities about the struggle for peace rang hollow (Johnston, 2006, 261–70). All of these issues particularly affected Estonians, as Estonia's proximity to the West made it one of the westernmost bases of the Soviet army (Laar and Hiio, 2018, 11).

The album's most anarchist-pacifist song, 'They Don't Know My Name', also pays homage to these themes. It reflects the contradiction between official rhetoric and reality in the Soviet Union, bringing together the forced militarism, the nuclear threat and the anarchist-pacifist rejection of the official policy. It is probably also the most complex song on the album, with music and lyrics complementing each other to form a new whole. Here, Villu Tamme sings from several positions – both anarchist-pacifist and in regard to the power structure. All of these layers are also expressed musically, with themes driven by different musical materials. As a result, the song lacks a square verse-chorus form, and various musical passages are woven into the song:

The minister doesn't know my name
If he knows anything at all
The minister is powerful and blind
Just as he's supposed to be

And he doesn't know my name
It doesn't interest him yet
The minister doesn't know my name
He doesn't know my name

The stars are twinkling above my head
The ground is covered by dust
Between my toes a little general
Stands and shouts: HOORAY!

They don't know my name
They haven't seen me yet
Even the general doesn't know my name
They don't know my name

The practice of destruction
Is the theory of creation
Everything starts anew
Do not be afraid of war, it's not the end of all
Everything starts anew

By singing 'The stars are twinkling above my head, The ground is covered by dust, Between my toes a little general, Stands and shouts: HOORAY!', Villu parodies Soviet militarism and official rhetoric, where ennobling peace went hand in hand with forced enthusiasm and its expression was expected at every level, from the common man to the head of state. By paraphrasing the rhetorical link between war and peace, he calls for people not to be afraid of war, a message which was utterly typical of official Soviet heroism. A good example here is the quote from one of the scientists who was working on the Soviet atomic project in the 1940s and 1950s: 'If you want peace, prepare for war.' In saying so, he showed how he saw his work on the bomb as contributing to Soviet and global security (Johnston, 2008, 267–9). Villu Tamme, too, paraphrases similar lines on a melodic contour which is reminiscent of the pioneer songs of the time in which people had grown up singing at school: 'Do not be afraid of war, it's not the end of it all. Everything starts anew.' However, melodically, J.M.K.E. uses reduced intervals, and the vivacious spirit of the pioneers takes on a mocking, even terrifying sound, which fits well with the anarchist perspective which is buried between the lines: 'The practice of destruction, is the theory of creation.'

In this song, the writer distances himself from the country's policy of militarizing people for armed conflict and taking them directly to the battlefield. It is worth remembering that when the lyrics were written, the Soviet-Afghan war was still ongoing. In this conflict, the ruling Marxist People's Democratic Party of Afghanistan was supported by the military forces of the SSSR. They were fighting the *mujahideen*, supported by foreign countries such as the United States and Britain. The Soviet Union intervened in 1979 in this conflict which began as a civil war in 1978 and left almost ten years later, on 15 May 1988. During those years, every young man in the Soviet Union was threatened by the war in Afghanistan. For most of them, it was an irrelevant and completely incomprehensible conflict.

At the same time, the lyrics of 'They Don't Know My Name' are undeniably poetic, the most poetic of all J.M.K.E.'s songs. By choosing the role of spectator and non-interventionist – 'Don't call me, I'm not in today. I locked up, went to see the battle' – the author distances himself from participating in conflict. The pioneering jumpy melody is replaced by a militant marching beat, and the singer subtly introduces the fear of the nuclear threat, which combines all fears into one: 'My initials are now flashing in the haze of nuclear winter, But the minister and the general won't know what they are.' He continues his static chant before returning to the usual hardcore punk, making it difficult for the listener to define where the irony ends and the actual feeling of pity begins: 'That wind, that silence, those colours – what a miracle! So beautiful is death and so stunning is the raped country, Pity they ever know my name, Nobody will ever know my name.'

Don't call me, I'm not in today
I locked up, went to see the battle
My initials are now flashing in the haze of nuclear winter
But the minister and the general won't know what they are
That wind, that silence, those colours – what a miracle!
So beautiful is death and so stunning is the raped country
Pity they ever know my name
Nobody will ever know my name

My name is Mindless War
My name is Famishing Hunger
My name is Violent Death
I was created by Man

They don't know my name
Not a single soldier, not a single ruler
Nobody knows my name
And there's no one to tell them

They don't know my name
Nor will they ever find out
They won't ever know my name

Phosphorite – no thanks!

Of all the songs, the author's green political thinking was most reflected in 'Hands Up, Virumaa', which combined it with a pacifist critique of power. In the USSR, with a green mindset, everything was in order on paper, and the Soviet Union actively created the image of a nature-preserving country. For example, in the second half of the 1950s and the early 1960s, the USSR enacted a wide range of environmental protection legislation, including the adoption of nature conservation laws and the establishment of national nature conservation agencies. More than any other country, the USSR was proud of its 'voluntary' nature conservation movement which was impressive on paper, with millions of people across the country belonging to nature conservation associations. At the same time, much of the environmental data and critical opinions about environmentally destructive projects, such as the diversion of Siberian rivers, were classified (Liivik, 2022, 132–3).

The 1980s saw the emergence of non-state environmental movements in many parts of the Soviet Union, which were linked closely to political activism. National goals and the desire to protect the environment were symbiotically linked (Kaljundi, 2022, 92–3). For example, the planned Daugavpils hydroelectric plant sparked discontent in Latvia in 1986, as did oil drilling in Lithuania in the same year, and the expansion of the Ignalina nuclear power plant two years later (Liivik, 2018, 124). The anti-nuclear movement also gained momentum in Ukraine and Russia after the Chernobyl nuclear disaster of 1986 (Dawson, 1996, 66–76, 99–100). J.M.K.E.'s song focuses on the ecological threat in Estonia, known as the Phosphorite War. It was a wave of protest which began in the winter of 1987 and culminated in the following spring in discontent against the establishment of phosphorite mines in Toolse and Kabala in Virumaa.

Back in 1983–4, no one believed that public opinion could prevent environmental pollution in Estonia. Three years later, it was public opinion which helped win the Phosphorite War. Moscow became interested in Estonian mineral resources as early as the mid-1970s when the proposition was to mine phosphorite in the region of Toolse. Estonian experts saw the danger to the environment and tried to slow the process, but these struggles did not reach the ear of the public. Toolse was only saved from mining because there were much larger phosphorite deposits in the regions of Rakvere and Kabala, and the authorities also wanted a deeper mine at the foot of the Pandivere plateau. In all, the Soviet Union's huge fertilizer industry needed the raw materials, so events continued to move towards the mines (Kaljuvee 2007).

All the while there remained active opposition to Moscow's plan from environmentalists, academics and even local politicians, all of which led to job losses. Public events began in February 1987, when the leading figures and journalists of the Estonian SSR gathered for a press conference to 'discuss problems of avoiding phosphorite deposits in the Rakvere region'. Juhan Aare, editor of the newspaper *Noorte Hääl*, presented a television interview with Yuri Yampol, the head of fertilizer production, who spoke openly about the plan by the Ministry of Mineral Fertiliser Production to mine in Toolse and Kabala and around Rakvere. This brought the issue to the awareness of the press and, from there, to civil movements and the streets (Veidermaa, 2009, 206–12; no author, 1987). That May, students marched in the university city of Tartu carrying the slogans 'A sober look at Virumaa' and 'Rest in peace, Kabala brachiopods', while people wore T-shirts with the slogan: 'You can't make bread from phosphorite', paraphrasing the common Estonian expression 'You can't make bread from shit'.

Today, the Phosphorite War is usually portrayed as the first stage in regaining independence. However, it was not only a fundamental struggle for freedom but also a clear response to a possible ecological threat in north-eastern Estonia. The aspect of national cultural identity was also central as, by the time of the Phosphorite War, Estonians had developed a strong sense of themselves as a people of nature – there has always been a lot of land covered with forest in Estonia, and it was common then, as it is now, to go mushrooming in the autumn and berry picking in the summer. Two factors came together: ecological and folkloric. As Kaljundi (2019) says, environmentalism re-emerged in Estonia in the 1960s, after the war and Stalinism, when it had become globally relevant, and Estonians began to value the forest as part of the national landscape. Mobility was a key factor. Public transport and cars made it easier to visit the forests, and nature tourism was actively being promoted. The roots of the self-image of Estonians as people of nature can also be traced back to the late Soviet era and the strengthening of the Finno-Ugric self-image as nature people. Similarly, when interest in ancient folk cultures and nature began to emerge in other parts of the world in the 1970s and 1980s, the Estonian Society for Nature Conservation (founded in 1966) was characterized by linking nature conservation closely to national culture and home studies.

All of these developments were reflected in real time by J.M.K.E.'s song, 'Hands Up, Virumaa'. The song encapsulated Estonian identity politics by resonating with the self-image of Estonians as a Finno-Ugric people of nature. But it also reflected the author's concern about possible environmental disasters and, as he said in an interview at the time, about the planet as a whole:

> What is there to rejoice about when we're sitting on a detonated bomb, and the fuse is already fizzing away. Can the forces of peace gather together enough to put it out in time? In the old days, war was probably an exciting game for some, an opportunity to demonstrate manhood for others. Organisers of wars could not yet make the whole world tremble. This is not the only reason for pessimism. The beautiful blue earth dries up, burns up, and dies even without wars. Man, who calls himself the king of nature, seems to hate in a panic the very nature which gave birth to him. He tortures and destroys his mother.
>
> (Haug, 1988, 34)

'Hands Up, Virumaa' combines several perspectives. From a lyrical point of view, the author does not clown about or attempt irony, but instead speaks openly about the matter which concerns him. In typical Tamme style, the lyrics combine direct and poetic self-expression. In the first verse, he reflects on the fear of foreign powers by weaving it into the cuckoo motif, the most popular bird in Estonian folk religion.

The cuckoo is also known as a bird of evil omen. If it sings near someone's home, it means someone's death, serious illness or fatal accident (Hiiemäe, 1996, 7). These different perspectives are also supported by the music. The song begins with a thick, jaunty guitar and beat, while the lyrics speak of possible doom:

> Strange faces moving about already
> Cuckoos calling destruction
> Abandon the country of your elders
> It's time to go and live in the woods
> In there, sitting in a spruce
> The cuckoo calls a hundred times
> Predicting hundred years of misfortune

In the second verse, the singer switches perspectives and becomes an occupier who repulses the natives and addresses them according to national stereotypes. At the same time, the tonality becomes more aggressive and the pretence of cheerfulness disappears:

> We don't drive you away
> But we think you should go
> Hands up, Virumaa
> Give us the phosphorite

And then, just as quickly, the writer switches back to the first person, speaking again from the point of view of an Estonian who is trying to protect nature. Aggressive music continues with a tight beat, only to suddenly slow down and paint a picture of what happens after the mineral resources are ruined:

Beneath the highland of Pandivere
The phosphorite lies hidden deep
The sluggish Estonian farmer
Only delays the mining work
Man of power, think again
Before you take that step
The people is against the phosphorite

In a farmyard, a well run dry
There's no reflection of a face
Only in winter can you quench your thirst
With water from melting snow

Hands up, Virumaa
Time to mine the phosphorite

In conclusion, the writer paints a naturalistic picture of a simple ecological disaster. He also returns to folklore by placing the final message in the mouth of a raven, a bird whose black plumage is associated with death and which folk religion considers to be the most unlucky of birds (Hiiemäe, 1996, 7). In the ever-accelerating rhythm, the writer weaves an ironic punch into the last lines of the song:

Then one morning a farmer stands
By his field of wheat
Tears flowing from his eyes
The field sinks under his feet
Dirty water washes the ears
A raven bellows on the top of a birch:
'You got it, you got it – but didn't get anything at all!'

The fertiliser has spoilt the soil
The fertiliser has spoilt the waters
But in the name of huge harvests
They still want more of it
Why don't you comrades produce more manure
Who'll need more fertiliser after that

The song's reception also reflected J.M.K.E.'s prominent position in Estonian society. In 1987, the live version of the song was used in the short movie – such clips were shown in cinemas before the main movie – to draw attention towards the acute danger of phosphorite mining. Punk music accompanies scenes of Estonian nature, interwoven with the composition 'Fratres' by the Estonian composer Arvo Pärt. When Tamme shouts: 'The people are against phosphorite!', the narrator continues, in a proper television announcer's voice: 'The band J.M.K.E. from Tallinn played at the All-Union Rock Festival in Podolsk.[1] Too emotional?' He leaves the answer to the expert: 'It turns out that this mining question is emotional. But it is still rational to use natural resources so that we do not spoil the rest of nature by opening a mine' (Tooming, 1987).

---

[1] The concert footage, however, was filmed in the stairwell of a house on the street of Harju in Tallinn.

5 'Hello Perestroika!' The Estonian punk movement at its peak

Perestroika scepticism

But the Soviet Union was still falling apart. Not immediately, but gradually, and from one moment to the next change was happening. By that time, the country was being governed by Mikhail Gorbachev, who had become the new leader of the Soviet Union in March 1985. Since Brezhnev and his successors had taken over, the Soviet Union had fallen into a hopeless spiral of economic crisis. The society was heavily influenced by corruption and alcoholism, something which was permeating all social classes from road workers to top officials. After the end of what became euphemistically known as the rule of the oldies, Gorbachev had to lead the country out of the crisis. He embarked on a programme of innovation which was designed to speed up the country's economic development and improve socialist society through restructuring: perestroika.

The opening shot was fired on 23 April 1985, when Gorbachev presented his vision to the plenum of the CPSU Central Committee in which the USSR's socio-economic development would be accelerated. This was also the beginning of glasnost, referring to the reduction of secrecy and the expansion of freedom of speech, an area of advancement which included disclosing crimes which had been committed by previous leaders, and a softening of censorship rules. People who, in fear of authorities, had learnt to censor themselves for decades began to speak out, at first quietly but then increasingly loudly, about injustices which had befallen their families (Made, 2011, 152–3).

The end of stagnation was agreed in the January plenum of the CPSU Central Committee in 1987, when perestroika was declared the country's official policy. The leading role of the communist party in the political life of the country began to diminish, and various social movements began to emerge alongside the single party, becoming the later political parties. Gorbachev also fundamentally changed Moscow's foreign policy. He abandoned the Stalinist bipolar world view, restrained the arms race which had exhausted the Soviet Union for many decades, and withdrew from regional conflicts – for example, by ending the war in Afghanistan. He also softened the confrontation between the USSR and the United States and the policy of non-interference in the Eastern Bloc, which ended with the 1989 demolition of the Berlin Wall, the symbol of the Cold War. The liberalization of Soviet political life and closer communications with the rest of the world in the following years, in some cases, prevented the Soviets from using explicit force against protests. The eyes of the world were on the Soviet Union. In summary, Gorbachev's policies shaped both the domestic and foreign policy framework which allowed Estonia to regain its independence in 1991, even if his goal was simply to give the Soviet Union a new lease of life (Tannberg, 2022).

While the West hailed Gorbachev's reforms as a manifestation of democracy, Estonians viewed them not only with joyful euphoria but also with some hesitation. Too often, the Soviet Union's official course had diverged from reality. It was during this period that the song 'To the Cold Land', was born, the angriest and boldest on the record. The album's title track, with several essential codes in it, perfectly sums up people's scepticism about change: the murderous Stalinist policy won't disappear but is instead waiting for its moment to return. The lyrics, cruelly and unadorned, reveal the tragedy of a small nation under foreign rule and cynicism towards the future and Gorbachev.

> Red flags are waving on a festive platform
> Gorby's waving his hand
> People are watching with amazement:
> 'What's that Gorby smiling at?'
> But Gorby's got a plan
> After the parade's over
>
> Perestroika will be over, too
> And we're all going to the cold land
> Singing in carriages a hymn to the homeland –
> To the cold land

In the fast-paced song the author angrily lists the national symbols of Estonians. 'Russian will become the language of Estonia,' he says, touching on decades of Russification and the fear of losing the nation's own language. 'And Dvigatel the headquarters,' he continues, referring to the local metal industry company. This was located in the Lasnamäe district and was considered a stronghold of the Russian-speaking population, while being directly linked to the anti-Estonian independence Intermovement. Its leaders continuously cooperated with the Union of Labour Collectives, which mobilized workers to take part in Intermovement rallies, strikes and demonstrations, as well as those of Dvigatel (Põlluste, 2019, 23–4).

Tamme continues: 'And Väljas [will be] a dissident, And Kogan [will be] the president. And dead behind the shithouse, lies Edgar Savisaar, Across the body of Marju Lauristin' – and all Estonians knew about what and whom he was talking. As secretary of the Estonian communist party between 1988 and 1990, Vaino Väljas led the party's reformation and skilfully participated in the Estonian independence movement. In 1988 he also led the adoption of the declaration of sovereignty of the Estonian SSR, which aimed to achieve sovereignty within the USSR. Edgar Savisaar and Marju Lauristin were leaders of the pro-Estonian independence Popular Front, while Jevgeni Kogan was one of the creators of the pro-Soviet Intermovement, whose loud rants against Estonian independence were familiar to the entirety of the Estonian people.

The lines also sound like a vulgar paraphrase of Soviet-era theoretical statements which denied the right of existence of nationalities as separate ethnicities within the Soviet Union. As the academician Aleksandr Holmogorov put it: 'As a result of the development of ethnic processes, the total number of peoples in the USSR is decreasing. The 1926 census recorded 194 ethnic names, while the 1970 census recorded no more than a hundred ethnic entities.' He then concluded with a completely arbitrary statement: 'The disappearance of names can be explained by natural, voluntary assimilation' (Kaasik, 2021, 54).

> Russian will become the language of Estonia
> And Dvigatel the headquarters
> And Väljas a dissident
> And Kogan the president
> And dead behind the shithouse
> Lies Edgar Savisaar
> Across the body of Marju Lauristin

But the song also refers to an immediate tragedy in the memory of Estonians: the March deportations, which were the most brutal act of violence against Estonians to be enacted by the communist regime. Between 25 and 28 March 1949, people from all of the Baltic states were forcibly resettled, mainly in Siberia. Over the course of four days, more than 20,000 people, mostly women and children, were loaded onto trains under armed guard, while hundreds were later sent to Siberia, and hundreds were born during the resettlement, of whom about 3,000 died in Siberia (Rahi-Tamm, 2005, 18–19). The entire song modulates musically, and the beat gets quicker when the singer focuses on a trace in the historical memory of Siberia about the transportation of Estonians there in animal carts. It reaches its climax in the chorus, when the music stops abruptly just as the singer shouts in a malevolent tone: 'To the cold land!', as if he's screaming out loud at a potential horror.

> Once again as prisoners will the Estonians ride
> Nothing to lose but a lot to win

We'll erect there a city that conceals the horizon
And build in Siberia the realm of Estonia again

The song also delves into deeper layers of memory than simply those of the Soviet deportations, quoting the novel by Estonian writer, Eduard Vilde *To the Cold Land* (1896). Estonians have a long history of being sent to Siberia, something which is also reflected in the novel. The main character, Jaan, is sent to a forced labour camp in Siberia in the nineteenth century, when Estonia was still a part of the Russian Empire, as a result of social injustice and poverty which leads an otherwise noble man down the wrong path.

How did it become possible to sing so honestly about these things? 'Then it already seemed that everything was really free. Not as free as later on, but certainly compared to before. But there was still no feeling that the Soviet Union would fall apart. That seemed impossible,' explains Villu Tamme. 'There was a constant feeling that they were doing something, whether Gorby's anti-drinking campaign, and then the [freer] news campaign, but it would end in failure anyway. Then the old Soviet Union would return, and there's no joke, when it does, and we would go to a cold land because we had become too bold too quickly.'

In the spirit of glasnost, 'To the Cold Land' was also broadcast on the TV, albeit in censored format with the names of Savisaar and Lauristin being censored but the word 'shithouse' not being cut out. According to the Tamme, this time, it was not Soviet censorship but pro-Estonian forces who wanted to prevent the names of star politicians being associated with a shithouse: 'It was funny. I don't know what people thought when such a rude word as "shithouse" was left in. What obscenities could be behind that beep' (Rinne, 2008, 47–8).

Similar feelings were expressed in the song 'The Streets of Tbilisi' (1989). In this musical act of solidarity, the writer looks at the capital of Georgia in the South Caucasus, 3,000 kilometres away from Estonia. The borders of both the Russian Empire and, later, the Soviet Union were drawn relatively arbitrarily and did not take into account the multi-ethnic composition of the South Caucasus. At the same time, these nations had not forgotten their short-lived independence as nation-states at the beginning of the twentieth century, or their former glory from earlier centuries. As a result, in the second half of the 1980s various ethnic groups in the region began to express a desire for greater autonomy, both in relation to each other and within the Soviet Union as a whole. One such protest took place on 9 April 1989, when people came to Tbilisi's central street – Rustaveli Prospect – to protest against Soviet rule (Kaas, 2011). Like other Estonians, Tamme read about what happened in Tbilisi by grabbing a newspaper – by this time so much more free in their content – which provided an honest and adequate picture: 'That same night the army, armed with shields, rubber truncheons, and sapper shovels, attacked the defenceless people. The hunger strikers were beaten, and poison gas was used. The crowd resisted. People died.' Altogether, twenty-one people were killed, including women and children, and hundreds were injured. As a result of the violence, protests continued and the entire country declared a general strike until the government which ran the Georgian SSR resigned (no author, 1989).

'The Streets of Tbilisi' kicks off immediately, carried by a steady beat and a strong guitar sound. The verse is characterized by a relatively minor soundscape, as well as augmented intervals and a wide melodic range, both of which make the song sound eerie. The song reflects not so much disappointment as a deep scepticism about perestroika, while Tamme straightforwardly declares that Georgia is not as far away as it might seem. Later in the interview he reflects on the lyrics: '[I was sure that] Estonian politics would not be tolerated for too long, and this nonsense would also reach us. Violence is right here, and it is naive to expect change':

> You're wrong to think that Tbilisi was an exception
> Totalitarian states have never been so bright
> The collapsing system will stop at nothing
> So don't hope for pardon, the soldiers aren't asleep
> They'll smash your skull with a sapper spade
>
> The government withdraws the army from abroad
> Soldiers from Mongolia, tanks from the DDR
> Obviously not to sit still at home
> But to keep the internal order of the state

The most significant change in the music occurs in the chorus, where the writer uses their usual technique of creating a sharp contrast between the music and the lyrics. As the beat thickens considerably and the harmony becomes strangely jolly, the singer paints a stark picture of what awaits people who dare to trust the system:

We'll see the streets of Tbilisi again and again
The spades are waiting to be used
People choking on gas again
We'll see the streets of Tbilisi again and again

The song ends by presenting the most likely future scenario which could await Estonians if they too decide to take to the streets. Here the singer uses one of his stylistic techniques, which is characteristic of first-person statement songs: almost in the form of conversational text, as if it has been spoken by one person to another:

Estonian politics won't be put up with for long
Freedoms will be restricted soon
If people lose their temper, they take to the streets
Where soldiers and tanks will be waiting for them

Don't put too much faith in democracy
The jackal is dressed up as the sheep of perestroika
Don't believe in pardon, the soldiers aren't asleep
They'll use their sapper spades to butcher you, too

Hello perestroika!

And then, out of this excitement, poverty and cynical weariness, came a singing revolution in Estonia. This was the umbrella term for a series of events which led to the restoration of independence from the Soviet Union for the Baltic states. In retrospect, the beginning of the Singing Revolution is often placed on 14 May 1988, during the annual, cutting-edge rock music event known as Tartu Music Days. On that day, Alo Mattiisen's 'Five Awakening Songs' was performed, a cycle which was inspired by the songs of the nineteenth-century national awakening and which was closely related to the tradition of the Estonian Song Festival. The Festival also dates back to the nineteenth century and the period of the first Estonian national awakening, with around 800 singers taking part in the first festival, and 22,600 today (no author, 1 June 2023). It also remained symbolic throughout the Soviet period, with a procession of singers walking through the streets of Tallinn to reach the Singing Square. Although the authorities tried to use the festival to their own advantage, it still carried the feeling of being a hidden passive protest (no author, no date).

Opinions vary when it comes to where the Estonian flag was first hoisted in public. Besides the Heritage Days in April 1988 (Tannberg, 2005, 379), the Tartu Music Days in May of the same year have been mentioned as potential claimants. As Latvian historian, Guntis Šmidchens, has put it (2014, 209), the non-conformist spirit of rock converged with explicit nationalism and civil disobedience when the audience unfurled two illegal Estonian flags. The next day, a sea of blue, black and white fluttered above the crowd. The flags were edited out of television broadcasts, but news of the revolutionary demonstration immediately spread. Three weeks later, during the next Old Town Days between 10 and 14 June, the flag was hoisted several times in various parts of Tallinn's Town Hall Square. At first the militia managed to take them down, until seven or eight rows of people gathered between the young flag-raisers and the militia, preventing the militia from coming near the flags. Anyone who attempted to take photographs of the young people, so that the authorities could blame them later, were also prevented from doing so (Rinne, 2007, 242). The Old Town Days became another decisive accelerator of events which would lead to the restoration of Estonian independence.

During the Singing Revolution, punk behaviour also became essential as punks allowed themselves to show publicly Estonian patriotism, thereby breaking with accepted behaviour in a socialist society. This is linked to another crucial series of events which had already begun a year earlier, on 4 June 1987. In the shadow of the Old Town Days, punks started singing Estonian patriotic songs together, first in Town Hall Square and then, after various forms of provocation for fights with the militia, in Singing Square. The spontaneous singing grew into the Night Song Festival, which reached its peak a year later with almost 300,000 participants. The local musical elite followed people to Singing Square to share in the singing of 'No Country Is Alone', or 'Let Us Go Up to the Hills (Stop Lasnamäe)' about back then largely Russianized area of Tallinn. Soon there were so many thousands of people dressed in blue, black, and white carrying ribbons and banners, and raising the colours up flagpoles, on walls, and on towers that the Soviets gave up trying to stop them (Šmidchens, 2014, 209). Why didn't the militia intervene? Because the news of the night singing festivals had already been broadcast abroad, and the credibility of perestroika would have suffered if tens of thousands of people had been attacked by tanks (Rinne, 2007, 243).

In Estonia, perestroika and the Singing Revolution are often associated with the solemn choral singing and national rock songs by the aforementioned composer Alo Mattiisen which provided the main sound for these events. The sentiments of the transition period were also summed up by the perestroika-era Rock Summer Festival, the first of which in 1988 and attracted 150,000 people over three days. It was well suited to the turbulent times and carried the motto 'Glasnost Rock – Rock for Peace'. The festival attracted artists from the other side of the Iron Curtain who found it exotic to perform in a previously closed Eastern Europe, including Public Image Ltd, Steve Hackett and Big Country (Lang, 2020). Another symbol of the era was a joint political demonstration by Estonia, Latvia and Lithuania a year later, on 23 August 1989. Wanting to show the world their desire for freedom and to draw attention to the Molotov-Ribbentrop Pact,[1] the people of the Baltic states formed a chain of about 2 million people, holding hands and stretching some 675 kilometres from Tallinn to Riga and from there to Vilnius.

Although rock music had been neglected for a long time during the Soviet era, by the end of the 1980s it had become institutionalized and, alongside official pop, the Singing Revolution also had a raucous soundtrack which was represented by punk. In the same decade, as Aimar Ventsel

---

[1] On the eve of the Second World War, on 23 August 1939, Germany and the Soviet Union signed an economic and political pact, the Molotov-Ribbentrop Pact. It was a non-aggression treaty between Germany and the USSR, with secret additional protocols which divided Europe into spheres of influence. As a result, the Soviet Union demanded permission to establish military bases in Estonia, which would receive many times more troops than stipulated in the agreement.

(2018) pointedly said, beaten-up down-at-heels became the heroes of perestroika. Incredible as it seemed, by 1988 the militia was no longer beating up punks, and the movement was providing the unofficial anthem to perestroika. 'Hello perestroika, democracy. A country is escaping the claws of dictatorship,' Villu Tamme sang in 1988 – and Estonians sang along. The song hit all levels of society, and the writer modestly believes that the song's mass appeal was one of the reasons for the Russian word 'perestroika' to become mainstream instead of the Estonian version. J.M.K.E. had become a superstar.

The sky is cloudless, the sea is blue
Everybody's breathing free and deep
Hammer and sickle are no longer a threat
Now they symbolise joyful work

Hello perestroika, democracy
A country is becoming free of dictatorship
Hello perestroika, hello happiness
The red flag isn't so horrible anymore

A tractor ploughs the field, trees bear fruit
Rahva Hääl [local newspaper] no longer lies
No more smoke coming from it's mouths
All the banned movies are shown
And the banned bands can raise their voice

Hello perestroika, democracy
It's great to say goodbye to dictatorship
Hello perestroika, hello freedom

Everybody's happily singing pioneer songs
Auu auu

The uniform of militia no longer sickens
Now it's nearly beautiful
You'll see militia and punks
Shaking hands in a friendly way

Hello perestroika, shooby dooby doo
The country now belongs to you and me
Every October is a great jubilee
The people celebrate: hurrah, hurrah, hurrah

In Virumaa not a well remains dry
An airship lands in front of a mausoleum [a reference to Lenin's
        mausoleum in Moscow's Red Square]
Well, what do you say?
The democracy is so great
That one can't but wonder

Hello perestroika, happy homeland
I'll say hello to you as long as I get you
Hello perestroika, democracy
Hello perestroika, give also your paw

In fact, according to Tamme, the change had already occurred a year prior, in 1987, when the song was written. This indicates, among other things, that the relationship between the punks and the militia had already shifted to 'a friendly way', as expressed in the song. At the start of 1987, Tamme recalls the final arrests due to their appearance: 'It was quite a breakthrough – a powerful sensation to walk freely down the street, although for years afterward, I would still feel a pang of fear upon seeing uniformed men approaching.'

Šmidchens (2014, 226–7) aptly analysed the phenomenon of 'Hello Perestroika' in which the first stanza proclaimed hyperbolically enthusiastic support for the new governmental campaign. But then, as if in passing, the song spoke the truth about the decades-long Soviet system: it was a dictatorship, not a democracy. The red flag was a symbol of a grisly violence. The newspapers lied. Films and music were banned. Punks were persecuted. If Soviet repressions truly were coming to an end then drunken jubilation was due. But at the very end of the song, Tamme expressed some doubts. 'I'll say hello to you as long as I get you,' he commented, hinting that perestroika was a sham. In conversational Estonian, the expression 'Give me your paw' was an informal, friendly invitation to shake hands, as if the two parties were friends in a bar. But the song's ironic tone redefined the phrase, instead reminding the public that it faces a dangerous partnership, possibly shaking hands with a wolf in sheep's clothing.

In the end, two versions of 'Hello Perestroika' were produced: the first softer and the second rockier. Initially, the soloist performed the song alone as an interlude at some concerts, but as the song gained popularity, a version with the light arrangement was also recorded. Later, a full-volume punk version was born, but as Tamme comments, such an approach did not fully justify itself:

It didn't fit at all with the idea where a naive person aspires to a happy future. In this song, I *was* a naive person, trying to sing a happy song with a happy face and a soft voice. I played a person who sincerely believes that a happy future has arrived. The song was also musically naive, playing single notes of the simplest rhythm in the world as if it were the first tune the person was singing – as if, for the first time in his life, he felt the need to pick up a guitar because life in the Soviet Union had suddenly become so beautiful.

The song is also musically ambivalent. It mocks the pioneer songs with which Soviet youths grew up, those which were full of optimism and belief in a bright future. A similar tone was parodied in the lyrics of 'Hello Perestroika'. But an attentive listener, someone who had the Soviet-era ability to read between the lines, could clearly sense that optimism and hope were being shadowed by the fear of possible disappointment, something which reflected the feelings of many young people at the time. As Tamme himself said in an interview for *Noorus* magazine in 1988, he did not believe in perestroika but also did not give up hope: 'It would turn out to be an overly positive society. But I am still in favour of perestroika. Something is changing.' At the same time, for the band, it was a surprise that 'Hello Perestroika' became such a hit. After all, it was just a song of mockery, one which was critical of the government, and there were many others like that at the time, as Villu remembers:

I wrote it at the kitchen table that night, along with two others. One was 'Secret Eyes', one of the first songs about KGB in 1987. Not much was known about their activity back then. The second one was a very silly song, and in the end, I tossed it into the corner. It was in the morning, around 10–11 o'clock, when some words came to my mind, like 'Hello perestroika'. I quickly wrote them down, and a funny verse came out. I played the beginning of [Finnish rock musician] Pelle Miljoona's song, 'Moottoritie on kuuma' [highway is hot – in Finnish], and the words came very quickly. Freddy [Grenzmann – soloist for Estonian punk band Psyhhoterror] came to visit, and I played him my three songs. Kont [guitarist of several punk bands, such as Verine Pühapäev and Velikije Luki] came, and some others too, and Freddy said: 'Oh, that last song is pretty cool!' The idea was that I'd sing it myself on the guitar between the other songs, so I sang it like that until the autumn. And then, for some reason, it became very popular.'

The author started to realize the magnitude of the song when he was invited to record it on the radio: 'I played it alone with a guitar, and soon heard it for the first time on the radio. Some verses had been censored. The verses which couldn't be used against the state were left in, and were combined with others, so the song was about half as long.' In retrospect, Tamme has noted that the song was also somewhat anachronistic because of its exaggerated optimistic irony, when there was already so much more freedom of speech than there had been a few years ago (Rinne, 2008, 131). This is not only a retrospective critique, and the author saw already back then these events with a mixed degree of humorous criticism:

In connection with the emergence of a 'new wave' in social life, we [punks] have actually become a mouthpiece for perestroika. In that sense, the feeling of 'mission' can be lost. Some punks are so annoyed that they're wondering what the point is of getting out and about in public if the police don't show up or arrest you anymore? (Haug, 1988, 33)

A similar scepticism about perestroika is reflected in 'Endless Saturday'. That was also supposed to be the title of the album, Villu recalls, but the record company preferred 'To the Cold Land': 'The thing is that "To the Cold Land" wasn't my idea, it was Vilde's, so it seemed out of place.'

In this song, performed almost entirely with a lively melody and to a similar rhythm, the writer mocks the Soviet government, parodying its rhetoric while speaking from its position. The singer reflects endless optimism, promising that everything will only get better, but ridicules the promises in the chorus by yodelling. At the same time, Tamme uses his usual absurd humour, promising that after an endless Saturday, there will be an endless Sunday. And finally, there will be a nuclear war, albeit a small one, but the Soviet man will forever carry the burden of building up a new society. Musically, the song has elements of rockabilly, almost mockingly utilized, with a fast guitar solo in dialogue with a rhythmic drumbeat, accompanied by harmonic modulations: a hint of where J.M.K.E. were heading in the future, becoming only ever more musically accomplished.

Democracy's coming closer day by day
Flags are waving as before, as they'll be waving even tomorrow
And there will be no war because the papers say a resolute
   'no' to war
And the army's defending us against treacherously smiling
   Reagan

Stalin is dead and the troubles are over
And Siberia's not threatening us
The sun will never set

And the endless Saturday will make everybody happier
I trust the telly, I trust the papers
I trust the army, I trust the party
My wonderful children will follow in my footsteps
There's a great future waiting for us

Life's an endless Saturday
And it will turn into an endless Sunday

Democracy's coming closer day by day
Flags are waving as usual, as they'll be waving even tomorrow
And there will be a nuclear war, the end of the world
But we have no fear
We'll be building a new society forever
There's a great future waiting for us
There's a great future waiting for us

Life's an endless Saturday
And it will turn into an endless Sunday

The journey to the album – A view from Finland

The album *To the Cold Land* was released by the Finnish record company Stupido Twins and Joose Berglund. Internationally, J.M.K.E. reached their peak with this album. But the opposite is also true – if there had been no J.M.K.E., there would be no Stupido Twins.

In November 1987, left-wing folk-punk legend Billy Bragg and three Finnish artists – Liisa Tavi, Tuomari Nurmio and

Kadotetut, as well as Estonia's Mahavok and ROSTA Aknad –
performed in Soviet Estonia, while foreign musicians continued
on to Moscow. At the weekend, Linnahall (the concert hall)
was too full for those who wanted to come in: 'On Saturday
and Sunday evenings a bridge of peace was built here with
the joint efforts of musicians of several nationalities,' noted the
cultural newspaper, *Sirp ja Vasar*, with decades of long and
firmly-established peace rhetoric. The article continued:

> An example of engaged music from England was provided by
> a young man from London, Billy Bragg, whose attacking voice
> and electric guitar did not spare the politics of the day . . . What
> was sung about in the Linnahall? About the tension between
> east and west, the injustice between east and west. They sang
> in many languages about a star, a star of hope which would
> illuminate the land of the people . . . The sonorous bridge
> of peace, becoming true with the joint agreement of the
> Estonian Republican Committee for the Protection of Peace
> and the city's governmental building in which musicians
> performed free of charge, with all of the proceeds being
> donated to the Peace Fund, will be completed this week in
> Moscow. (No author, 1987)

The article does not mention the fact that, along with Bragg
and the Finnish musicians, journalist Joose Berglund, who was
in his early twenties, arrived in Estonia. Berglund had been
interested in Estonia for a long time: 'By that point the word
had started to get out that something big was happening
in there and that it was not just a stagnant little state in the
Soviet Union.' Since Berglund was working as a journalist
for the Finnish music magazine *Rumba* and the newspaper

Iltalehti, he offered to accompany the musicians on the trip, 'as a bloody roadie if nothing else', Berglund recalls. He ended up writing several articles about the trip.

At the same time, an underground concert with the same musicians took place in *Kinomaja* (Cinema House), where Velikije Luki and J.M.K.E. also performed. 'It was really fresh and exciting – like getting back to *Lepakko*, the occupied house here in Helsinki [which existed between 1979 and 1999], the home of the punk scene in the early 1980s, where it all started', Joose recalls what fascinated him about Estonian punk. On this trip, in the lobby of the Viru Hotel where Finnish tourists used to stay, Berglund met Villu who, according to his memories, was talked about in Estonia as being the king of the punks: 'I was probably trying to buy some stamps or whatever. I knew who he was, and he suddenly came over and asked me for a cigarette. I didn't have one because I didn't smoke then, but we ended up chatting. He spoke really good Finnish, so it was easy to communicate.'

Berglund had no plan to start the Stupido Twins record company:

> We were just young adults, hanging around, having fun. We had energy, and we had met these great people in Estonia. So obviously we wanted to make things happen for them as well, so that they could come to Finland. We tried to organise gigs for them, especially for Villu, but he wasn't able to get a visa because J.M.K.E. was considered a bad example of Soviet youth.

But by then the concert had already been set up, on 5 December 1988. The venue was a small restaurant next to the *Lepakko* squat, where the local punk rock youths used to hang out, and the clientele mainly consisted of older customers until youths took over the place. At first, DJ music was played until those involved came up with the idea of organizing concerts, remembers Berglund: 'So we decided to start the Finnish-Estonian friendship evening, a bit like the Russian friendship thing.'

When it became clear that visas were being refused, the organizers decided: 'Fucking hell, we'll run the show anyway with Finnish bands and give the money to the Estonians.' As the concert was taking place on the night before Finnish Independence Day, everyone had the next day off, and the event was very popular. The organizers sold out the place – 250 tickets – and got a reasonable amount of money back from it. Berglund recalls: 'So we promised to give the money to the Estonian youth, but what can you do? You can't put the money in an envelope, write "to the Estonian youth" on it and put it in the letterbox. We had to invent something else.'

From a trip to Estonia, Berglund had a demo tape of J.M.K.E. and another punk band Ba-Bach. Together with Jorma Ristilä, Berglund devised the idea to print some singles. In early 1989 the singles were ready, so the concerts in Finland could start in April and the album followed in November. J.M.K.E. turned out to be successful, despite the difficulty in getting the band to Finland. 'The time was perfect. Here was the bloody revolution. [The Estonian indie band] Röövel Ööbik got a visa because they were not as dangerous to the system as J.M.K.E. probably was: Villu was considered a political person,' recalls Berglund when contacting Hannu Puttonen of the Finnish communist party's youth magazine. There was a big celebration coming up: the bicentenary of the French Revolution. This was marked by a spectacular meeting called Left Forum *Vasemmistofoorumi*, which brought together many left-wing parties and movements. It was accompanied by a festival at the House of Culture in Helsinki, a venue which could hold 1,500 people. After a party meeting and seminars, there was an evening party and J.M.K.E. seemed to be the perfect guest to play for the members of the Finnish Communist Party. Villu Tamme remembers that the invitation to perform at the festival was delivered to his door by some leftist Finnish politician, so the Soviet authorities were forced to accept it – it was basically as if it were a 'pro-Soviet' party.

So finally, in late April 1989, the concert happened. Because of the party conference, all of the Finnish media was there. During the day, Villu sang 'Hello Perestroika' alone in the congress hall between speeches, which was also shown on the evening news, and in the evening, he performed with J.M.K.E. and local bands at the event party. Joose recalls:

And suddenly, there is an Estonian punk rock guy singing 'Hello perestroika'. So if you know how the media works, who's gonna be the face of that happening? Who was the guy on the front page of *Helsinki Sanomat*, the main newspaper in Finland? Who was the guy on the TV news and in all the other magazines? It was not the party chairman, it was the Estonian punk rocker in his ripped jeans and leather jacket.

6 'Endless Saturday'
J.M.K.E. in the midst of different ideologies

As an historian, throughout the writing of this work, I have tried to place J.M.K.E.'s own work within a larger narrative. An essential part of the process was correspondence with the author, Villu Tamme, who read over the manuscript and commented on it. 'You've analysed it quite interestingly', he wrote after reading another section. 'At times, it feels like an epic or a musical stage play, with so many different facets and meanings, when in fact it's just a bunch of laconic song lyrics. But, oh well, that's basically what's behind all these lines, so there's nothing wrong with that.'

The author was being modest here, in fact, because all these meanings were also intuitively read into the album by the audience without any further considerable analysis. The songs also spoke to people of different generations with their abstract anarchist message, wrapped up in a gripping musical form, regardless of the current governmental regime. One such song is 'The Solution Is Chaos'. Although the song was not on the album, it can be found on a B-side of the single 'Hello Perestroika'.

One layer of the song is how the idea of a change of power has become realistic, but, despite external optimism, people cannot overcome their deep pessimism. Even when promised a complete system overhaul, their hopelessness does not leave them. It is cynical to offer perestroika as a solution because that comes from above – from those in power – and, as Tamme sings, 'perestroika was not the initiative of the people'. The change in power, in all likelihood, means only replacing one regime with another of the same kind. And while the song is clearly set within the context of perestroika, to the ears of the audience, it is easily adaptable to any regime or government, whether social-democratic or national-conservative, or whoever, and, in the end, people may still feel left alone. That is why the only solution for them is anarchy, where there is no power distribution and no one controls anyone's rights.

Neither Russia nor a foreign land offers emotions
There is no difference between all these systems
No statesman has fulfilled the will of the people
He only uses the state to consolidate his position

This song also delicately outlines the reason for J.M.K.E.'s success with such a diverse group of people. Often, their lyrics are abstract enough to touch upon the universal personal experiences and dissatisfactions. For example, the song is also well suited to describe the mood which prevailed after the fall of the Soviet Union. The collapse was a solution, and what followed was chaos. It is precisely this ambiguity which makes J.M.K.E. so understandable to completely different groups: left-wing, right-wing and apolitical ones, regardless of age or gender. The fact that the song is a powerful statement is also underlined by the melody, which is remarkably different from other songs. The musical material is scarce, and Villu Tamme sings the chorus text mainly on a single, ascending melodic contour which is introduced to the listener in the guitar intro:

> I don't believe in any flag
> I don't believe in any coat of arms
> It's a machination
> It's not a solution
> It's not a solution (the system is still the same)
> It's not the solution (the state is not the solution)
> It's not a solution (chaos's the solution)

After a vigorous statement, the singer switches to an ironically mocking stance. Guitars are replaced by a lilting, childlike electric organ, whose cheerful chords symbolize a crowd of people who don't think with their heads:

> Everyone's hands are shaking and their minds are tense
> A great country has been taken over by perestroika mania
> But look – the system is the same
> Perestroika is nothing but a new campaign
>
> People, do you think there's freedom now?
> A divine light is shining from the shadow of a great leader
> Perestroika was not the initiative of the people
> But the people run after it like a flock of sheep
>
> I don't believe in Gorbachev
> I don't believe in perestroika

All these reforms
Are a grandiose fraud

And it's not a solution
The solution is chaos (a power-free society)
The solution is chaos (liberated mankind)
The solution is chaos (ideal society)
The solution is chaos

Must be torn from the confines of the system
Abolish all forms of legal control
People will go straight to the bottom if they are stupid
If they're clever, it will be the best of all states.

Just a few years after releasing *To the Cold Land*, Estonia became free. National ideas, national unity and the Singing Revolution which brought people together were replaced by cowboy capitalism in conditions of complete poverty. Many wanted to get rich at once, by whatever means. Crime flourished as the structures of power needed to be rebuilt. Groups from as far away as the South Caucasus and closer to home in Russia arrived in Estonia, and also local gangs emerged. Stalls flourished with smuggled alcohol and cigarettes alongside pirate cassettes from Poland, and the gangs settled scores.

There was no work, no money and the shops were empty, except for the currency shops where goods that could not be bought in a regular shop were sold for foreign currency. The cupboards in people homes were piled high with washing powder and soap, salt and other shortages, enough perhaps to provide for the next twenty years. 'It was that disgusting brown laundry soap. All the soap and other rubbish had piled up in the houses, mainly thanks to the coupon system[1] – no one had time to use up the piles of soap they could buy for coupons. But they bought it anyway in bulk. That's human nature,' also Villu Tamme recalls. There is much more to remember such as how neon jackets replaced the red pioneer scarves. Or the desire for Adidas sneakers, which could be replaced by cheap copies on the market with the label 'Adidos'. An ice cream parlour known as Penguin opened its doors on Town Hall Square a few years before the break-up of the Soviet Union. Estonian children had never had ice cream like this before, straight from the ice cream machine, brown on one side and blue on the other! Finnish ice cream, we thought, perhaps because we were used to thinking that all good and tasty things come from there. Legend says that, at first, the queues ran halfway across the square. For many of my generation, it was the ice cream with the penguin logo which, strangely, marked the triumph of early capitalism in 1990s Estonia.

All of this social turmoil found its expression in punk. While Estonian punk in the 1980s was strongly ideologized in terms of its anti-communism, in the 1990s its members were more concerned with abstract dissatisfaction with a rapidly changing society which seemed to be heading in an unknown direction. This is also reflected in J.M.K.E.'s next album, *Culture of Gringos* (1993), which is a sharp social critique of the blossoming early capitalism in Estonia, as one of the verses of the new album's title track suggests:

---

[1] At the end of the Soviet years, due to the deficit, coupons were needed in addition to real money to buy certain consumer goods.

We've got novel ethics now
Tactics of westernisation
To our country is coming the culture of the gringos
The scoundrels wearing ties
Are carrying the new culture
They have long ago got free
From the remorse for foreign currency
My republic has deceived me
My republic has no price

The 1990s are considered a rather difficult time for Estonian rock music. Some more prominent bands were still active, but many ceased to exist under the new circumstances. When Urmas Alender, the most famous rock musician, was lost in the 1994 MS Estonia ferry disaster, taking the lives of 852 people on their way from Tallinn to Stockholm, it symbolically marked the low point for Estonian rock. In Estonian punk the era is also often remembered as a low point. Punk, the strongest subculture of the 1980s, was going through a kind of identity crisis. By the beginning of the new decade, the controlling foreign power had disappeared, and many punks had simply grown older.

Yet it is arguable whether it is right to speak of a low point in punk. Yes, punk was no longer in the mainstream charts, but the question was whether it should ever have to be there. As Villu Tamme said, punk was back where it belonged, in the niche or alternative landscape which was, on the other hand, effervescent during those years. After all, mental and geographical borders were opening up, and people were much freer to experiment with different identities, including musical ones. Tamme had expressed similar thoughts about punk a few years earlier in response to whether it was pop (no author, 1988, 4): 'Punk shouldn't be a fashion thing at all. Punk is a movement. Its true content becomes clear when you have been a punk for at least a few years. Punk doesn't expire as long as someone [who consider itself] punk still exists somewhere.'

Now, in the final chapter, it's time to remember that I was a child of the 1990s. And as a member of the punk scene at the time I didn't realize that there was anything wrong with it. Punk – and subcultures in general – were very much part of the urban landscape because there was no longer a police system to chase us away. Concerts remained full, as they still are in 2023. Events were happening all the time, sometimes directly in the street and, despite the general post-Soviet poverty, we always managed to find money for the tickets. And although many new bands were formed, J.M.K.E. remained the crucial one. The act of writing down history sometimes leaves the impression that there was a sudden disruption in 1991, with a clear division between the 'before' and 'after' in terms of the start of the Second Estonian Republic. In reality, the borders were blurred. The previous era's ideas, clothes and culture were not thrown away overnight and replaced by new ones. As a result, much of the music young people listened to in the 1990s also came from the previous decade. One such record was J.M.K.E. *To the Cold Land*. I also know that demand outstripped supply because, for several years, I used to go to the National Library after school to listen to the record with headphones on. Music was not so freely available to youths back then, and that was the only chance many had to be able to listen to some of their favourite bands, as many of us did not even have tape recorders at home. Often, there was a queue for the record because three other mates, who had probably already finished their lessons ahead of me, were already there, either listening to the record or waiting to listen.

Society calmed down in the early years of the twenty-first century, and middle-class values became prevalent. After the anti-Soviet 1980s and the deideologized 1990s, the start of the new century brought with it fresh upheaval. In the 2000s, subculture became clearly ideologized. Some people defined themselves as Antifa, while others where right-wing punks or remained apolitical. Nowadays, the Estonian punk movement is characterized by its internal polarization, with both left-wing and right-wing punks being vocally present. In the midst of all that, J.M.K.E. and its vocalist, Villu Tamme, have remained symbols of Estonian punk.

I have been particularly intrigued by how they had done it. With that thought in mind, and while writing this chapter, I invited people on social media to reflect upon why they listen to J.M.K.E. and what world view they associate with it. The post was widely shared, and I was contacted by strangers so that I ended up speaking to boys and girls who were aged between eleven and thirteen, men in their fifties and people in their thirties and forties. Three main narratives emerged from these discussions. The older generation had experienced the birth of the album in real time and among them many (but not all) saw it as a powerful statement against the Soviet occupation. The album also spoke to a longing for the national values at the time at which power changed hands, and the patriotic message was amplified, especially when living outside Estonia. For example, a man who joined the punk scene in 1985 thought this was the most anti-communist album by J.M.K.E. and the Eastern Bloc countries.

Compared to the previous generation, the educational aspect of the album had a more significant impact on the youth of the 1990s. At a time in which school and teachers were dull and unexciting, or the academic approach to history was too national-romantic for the cynical post-Soviet youth, the record offered them an alternative school lesson through Estonia's recent communist past. As Heiko recalls:

> For me, J.M.K.E. was where I gained knowledge about so many things, from history to religion. Since I was very interested in history, I researched everything written in the songs of *To the Cold Land*. I sensed from their music that the Soviet Union was bad and oppressive. And the music and the words were equally important. Since the cassette which had been released by [cooperative] Kuldnokk did not contain the lyrics, I went to the library to copy them down from Villu's poetry collection, 'Pigeon was a titmouse'. I sat there with my headphones on and sang along in my head. The music was so mesmerising, and I listened so loudly that finally, I got a letter of reprimand from the ladies in the reading room.

The record's educational aspect is also emphasized by today's youth. However, whereas the older generation created a clear historical narrative which was based on the record, education was more instinctive and not necessarily so political for today's kids. 'These songs provide so much information about life and everything else. From this album you get the greatest amount of life wisdom, even if you don't understand it at first,' thirteen-year-old Mona wrote me. In the same way, the young audience caught onto the album's anarchist message, as Miia Maria said: '"Summer of the white butterfly" [is one of my favourite songs] because it's catchy and thoughtful. "They don't know my name" has a very "punk" meaning.' The anarchist idea also appealed to its audience of forty-year-olds and, in the twenty-first century, green politics and an anti-war mindset have become even more topical, especially within the context of today's war in Ukraine, as Astrid expresses: 'From a world view – live and let others live. And the whole of J.M.K.E's creation for me is definitely to consume less.'

Regardless of age or gender, the audience emphasized the musical side of the album. For example, twelve-year-old Herta Ida says: 'The great thing about it is that you feel the music taking you along from the very start. It just has such a cool vibe.' Heiko offers an analytical view of his early youth in the 1990s:

> The eclecticism of this music confused me greatly. Everything was constantly changing, and it seemed very much the opposite of what was coming out on the radio at that time. The drum part was a benchmark for Estonian punk drummers in the nineties and 2000s. Lots of breaks. . . . In terms of guitar and bass, of course, very few reached this level. . . . This album defined the main trends in Estonian punk.

All in all, during the correspondence, I realized that what I was trying to prove with the book was already intuitively clear to listeners. When looking for common denominators in the background of this captivating music, the abstract feeling of the *To the Cold Land* album is that the music confronts evil, even if what is understood as evil depends on the listener: for some, it is communism and totalitarianism, or the destruction of the planet by man, while for others, it is the sacrifice of human beings for a noble idea. In this way, J.M.K.E. demonstrates the timelessness of what they were saying in 1989; it remained relevant in the following decades, whether to the late or post-Soviet youth, or to the children of the new century who do not feel connected to the Soviet past. So, to an extent, J.M.K.E. is the historical memory of Estonians, one which spans generations. The album offers an opportunity to remember as an active act of reconciliation between past and present. The meaning of the past in relation to the present is what is at stake here. As often in such cases (Keightley, 2010, 58), those memories coherently bring into each other's view our changing sense of who we are and who we were.

After all that, what can be said here as a conclusion? J.M.K.E. didn't stop in 1989 with their first album but continued to make music. And they did it well, always capturing the essence of what was in people's minds at the time. They criticized the early capitalism that left many people confused in a time of transition, cunningly ironized the self-destructiveness of young punks, and, as early as 1996, articulated the role of the internet as both a unifier of people and an amplifier of loneliness. I remember being particularly struck by their song 'The Future Is an Hour Away', written during the years when Estonia became independent. Those lines reflect the state of affairs after the rapid change of government. But I also remember the song always, whenever I experience a significant change in my life. It has turned out that not just me – anyone can easily relate to it (and J.M.K.E. in general), be it the transition from adolescence to adulthood or a more drastic event which forces us to reassess our lives. I believe that the timelessness which shines through these lines sums up the reason the band is so important across generations of Estonians.

Future is in an hour
Culture of Gringos, 1993

I'm not sure who I am anymore
I'm not anymore who I was
Do I have to be who I want to be
Or do I have to be who I am somewhere at my core?

And what will come somewhere in the mute future
I haven't even an hour left to think it over
Because future is in an hour

I'm not any rebel anymore
But I don't agree with anything yet, too
I still want to change some things
But I already distrust my strength

And the future is in an hour
I've got an hour to think about the future
And on my strength

I'm not sure who I am anymore
My intellect is limited by my hair
But when I shave off half of my scalp
I understand completely nothing

And then I take a vodka from my corner cupboard
And mix it with tomato juice
And then I know all the truth right away

My past is the folly of my own
My future is the sweetest dream of mine
My present is some weird substance
And it lasts till every new morning

And the future is in an hour
The future will be there in the morning
Or even sooner
Even today

Everything's right what's done in the past
And the present day is even more so
My future is in my own hands
And it will be the only right one

I create my future myself
And my Destiny helps me to create it a little bit, too
Quite a trifle
So I live in my dreams.

And in some level in my memories too
My future is in my own hands
But knowing this won't make me wise

Illustrations

'I only became aware of punk in 1978 because there was not much information or music available during the Soviet era. I had read about it in *Suosikki* (a Finnish magazine). There were record sales tables, prices on the back and all kinds of advertisements. Then there was punk rock and I thought, 'What does that mean?' The name 'Sex Pistols' was in front of my eyes. I was confused and I couldn't relate it to anything. I thought maybe it was like Boney M., popular but maybe sexier with more naked women singing. But then my classmate gave me a Pistols sticker and I thought, "Oh! I want to be like that!" That's how it went.'

Photo credit/courtesy of Ardo Ran Varres.

Many punk concerts were banned in Soviet Estonia, and posters were taken down. This poster was made by Villu Tamme and put up by J.M.K.E. drummer Venno Vanamölder, who rode around the surrounding villages on his motorbike. Later, a militiaman drove along the same road on a motorcycle and removed them all.

Artwork credit/courtesy of Villu Tamme.

'I was relatively indifferent at the time, letting them do what they wanted. It seemed a temporary thing which nobody would remember in a few years. But for some reason, it's still remembered today, and that's why I'm still suffering from all sorts of things which were done behind my back, from the front cover of *To the Cold Land* to the hundreds of typos in the lyrics. Can anyone like an album cover with their own stupidly smiling face on it? I don't think that even pop or *schlager* musicians like it; they just must follow that style.

'But on the cover of a punk album with a strong political message, it's utterly ridiculous, unrelated to the content and utter crap.'

Photo credit on the first cover: Pentti Hokkanen.
Artwork credit on the second cover: Villu Tamme.
Courtesy of Stupido Records.

IV

To the Cold Land, centerfold of the album.
Courtesy of Stupido Records.

Bibliography

Ambrosch, Gerfried. 'Punk as Literature: Toward a Hermeneutics of Anglophone Punk Songs'. In *AAA: Arbeiten Aus Anglistik Und Amerikanistik* 42/1 (2017): 101–20.

Anstett, Élisabeth. 'An Anthropological Approach to Human Remains from the Gulags'. In *Human Remains and Mass Violence: Methodological Approaches*, edited by Élisabeth Anstett and Jean-Marc Dreyfus, 181–98. Manchester: Manchester University Press, 2014.

Colegrave, Stephen and Chris Sullivan. *Punk. Hors limites'.* Paris: Éditions du Seuil, 2002.

Danaher, William. 'Songs of Social Protest, Then and Now'. In *Songs of Social Protest*, edited by Aileen Dillane, Martin Power, and Amanda Haynes, 63–74. Lanham, MD: Rowman and Littlefield, 2018.

Davidjants, Brigitta. 'Identity Construction in Narratives: Activists of the Armenian Diaspora in Estonia'. In *Armenians in Post-Socialist Europe*, edited by Konrad Siekierski and Stefan Troebst, 129–42. Vienna and Cologne: Böhlau Verlag, 2018.

Davidjants, Brigitta. 'Naised Tallinna Pungis'. *Müürileht*, 20 June 2021.

Denisoff, Serge and Richard A. Peterson. 1972. *The Sounds of Social Change*. Edited by Serge Denisoff and Richard A. Peterson. Chicago: Rand McNally, 1972.

Dillane, Aileen, Martin J. Power, Eoin Devereaux, and Amanda Haynes. 'Introduction: Stand up, Sing Out: The Contemporary

Relevance of Protest Song'. In *Songs of Social Protest*, edited by Aileen Dillane, Martin J. Power, Eoin Devereux, and Amanda Haynes, 1–10. International Perspectives. New York: Rowman & Littlefield, 2020.

Dovlatov, Sergei. 'Vertikaalne linn'. *Looming* 8 (1998): 1171–88.

Goure, Leon. 'Soviet Exploitation of the "Nuclear Winter" hypothesis'. 5 June 1985.

Guerra, Paula and Henrique Grimaldi Figueredo. 'Today Your Style, Tomorrow The World: Punk, Fashion and Visual Imaginary'. In *ModaPalavra E-Periódico* 12/23 (2019): 112–47.

Haug, Jürgen. 'J.M.K.E'. *Noorus* 7 (1988): 33–4.

Hiiemäe, Mall. 'Nelikümmend lindu Eesti rahvausundis'. In *Mäetagused* 1/2 (1996): 7–23.

Hiio, Toomas. 'Dissidendid ja psühhiaatria: Peter Reddaway mälestused NSV Liidust ja Nõukogude teisimõtlejatest'. In *Propaganda, sisseränne ja monumendid, Eesti Mälu Instituudi toimetised*, 227–38. Tartu ja Tallinn: Tartu Ülikooli ja Eesti Mälu Instituut, 2021.

Johnston, Timothy. 'Peace or Pacifism? The Soviet "Struggle for Peace in All the World", 1948-54'. In *The Slavonic and East European Review* 86/2 (2008): 259–82.

Käär, A. 'Kadunud on tuumapomm'. *Säde: lasteleht* 11 (5 February 1966): 3.

Kaas, Kaarel. 'Veretu lagunemise müüt'. *Rahvusvaheline Kaitseuuringute Keskus* (2011): 100.

Kaasik, Peeter. 'Psühhiaatrilise sundravi kuritarvitamisest Nõukogude Liidus'. In *Tuna* 4 (2011): 79–96.

Kaasik, Peeter. 'Suunatud migratsioon Eestisse Teise maailmasõja järgsel perioodil'. In *Propaganda, sisseränne ja monumendid, Eesti Mälu Instituudi toimetised*, 49–88. Tartu ja Tallinn: Tartu Ülikooli ja Eesti Mälu Instituut, 2021.

Kagovere, Ott. 'Shifting Identities in Estonian Punk and Hip-hop'. In *Hopeless Youth*, edited by Francisco Martínez, 78–83. Tartu: Estonian National Museum, 2015.

Kaljundi, Linda. 'Eestlus – loodusrahvamüüt keskkonnakriisi ajastul'. *ERR*, 9 August 2019.

Kaljundi, Linda. 'Kunst, keskkond ja keskkonnaliikumine Eestis 1960.–1980. aastatel – mõningatest hästi unustatud seostest ja suundumustest'. In *Methis* 24/30 (2022): 92–116.

Kaljuvee, Ardo. 'Fosforiidisõda päästis Kirde-Eesti looduse pöördumatust hävingust'. *EPL*, 26 May 2007.

Keightley, Emily. 'Remembering Research: Memory and Methodology in the Social Sciences'. *International Journal of Social Research Methodology* 13/1 (2010): 55–70.

Kiin, Sirje, Rein Ruutsoo, and Andres Tarand. *40 kirja lugu*. Tallinn: Olion, 1990.

Kotta, Kerri, et al. *Eesti muusikalugu*. Manuscript. Tallinn: Eesti Muusika- ja Teatriakadeemia kirjastus [to be published].

Kreegipuu, Tiiu. 'Ajakirjandus Nõukogude Eestis külma sõja võitlusvahendina. Nõukogude Eesti Külma sõja ajal'. In *Nõukogude Eesti külma sõja ajal*, edited by Tõnu Tannberg, 163–99. Tartu: Eesti Ajalooarhiivi Toimetised, 2015.

Kuldkepp, Mart. 'Vene sõjaväe eestlastest desertöörid Esimese maailmasõja ajal Rootsis'. *Ajalooline Ajakiri* 155/1 (2016): 9–40.

Kümmel, Toomas. 'Valikud, mida polnud: Toomas Kümmel tutvustab II Maailmasõjas kahte vastaspoolel sõdinud venda ning nende saatust'. *Keskus*, 29 November 2004.

Laar, Mart. *Metsavennad. Relvastatud vastupanu Eestis Teise maailmasõjajärel*. Tallinn: Read, 2013.

Laar, Mart and Toomas Hiio. *Eesti riigi 100 aastat. I osa*. Tallinn: Post Factum, 2018.

Laugen, Lauri. 'Dmitri Medvedev Kaja Kallasele: see, et olete vabaduses, pole teie teene, vaid meie puudujääk'. *Delfi*, 9 August 2022.

Lieberman, Robbie. *'My Song Is My Weapon': People's Songs, American Communism, and the Politics of Culture, 1930-1950.* Illinois: University of Illinois Press, 1989.

Liivik, Olev. 'Glasnost Policy Reaching Estonia: Fear and Hope in the Protest Letters of Estonian Residents during the Campaign against the Phosphorite Mines in 1987'. In *The Baltic States and the End of the Cold War* , edited by Kaarel Piirimäe and Olaf Mertelsmann, 123–55. Berlin: Peter Lang, 2018.

Liivik, Olev. 'Vastuseisust protestideni: võitlus fosforiidikaevanduste vastu 1970. ja 1980. aastate Eestis'. In *Methis Studia humaniora Estonica* 24/30 (2022): 132–55.

Made, Tiit. *Kaks korda iseseisvaks. Eestlaste 20. sajandi pöördepunktid.* Tallinn: Argo, 2011.

Maripuu, Meelis. 'Külma sõja aegsed näidiskohtuprotsessid Eesti NSV-s: õigus ja propaganda kaalukausil'. In *Nõukogude Eesti külma sõja ajal, Eesti Ajalooarhiivi toimetised 23*, 88–140. Tartu: Rahvusarhiiv, 2015.

McRobbie, Angela. *Postmodernism and Popular Culture.* London and New York: Routledge, 2005.

Mertelsmann, Olaf. 'Külma sõja algusaja majanduslikud ja sotsiaalsed tagajärjed Eesti NSVs'. In *Nõukogude Eesti Külma sõja aja*, 141–62. Tartu: Eesti Ajalooarhiiv, 2015.

Miil, Marek. 'Kommunistliku partei propagandastrateegiad'. In *Ajalooline ajakiri* 1, 79–110. Tartu: Tartu Ülikooli Kirjastus, 2013.

No author. 'Põgenejad'. *Eesti Sõna* 233, 9 October 1943, 1.

No author. 'Võta või lapse vitsad'. *Sirp ja Vasar*, 7 June 1957, 7.

No author. 'Puhtal pinnal torkab silma must plekk'. *Sirp ja Vasar*, 28 June 1957, 7.

No author. 'Aatomisurma ohule astub vastu rahvaste üksmeelne tahe'. *Hiiumaa Rajoonikomitee ja Hiiumaa Rajooni Töörahva Saadikute Nõukogu häälekandja* 128/1501, 30 October 1958: 1.

No author. 'Tuumapomm ja vaimne tervis'. *Ühistöö : Rapla maakonna ajaleht* 15, 2 February 1963, 4.

No author. 'Isegi Moskva hipid kipuvad Tallinna'. *Vaba Eesti Sõna*, 24 August 1972, 3.

No author. 'Kreml ründab soome TV:d Õhtulehes'. *Eesti Päevaleht*, 20 October 1982, 1.

No author. 'Fosforiidi kaevandamise probleeme'. *ERR*, 31 March 1987, https://arhiiv.err.ee/audio/vaata/fosforiidi-kaevandamise -probleeme. Accessed 29 August 2023.

No author. 'Rahusild'. *Sirp ja Vasar*, 27 November 1987, 2.

No author. 'Levi lemmik. JMKE'. *Säde* 51, 25 June 1988, 4.

No author. 'Ajaloopärimuse küsimustik'. *Saarte Hääl*. 7, 19 January 1989, 3.

No author. 'Tbilisi ärevad päevad'. *Kodumaa*, 19 April 1989, 2.

No author. 'Üldlaulupeod 1869–2019'. *Eesti Laulu- ja Tantsupeo Sihtasutus*, No date.

No author. '14. juunil rahvuslik meeleavaldus ja mälestuskoosolekud Tallinnas'. *Meie Kodu*, 29 June 1988, 1.

Noor, Heino. 'Tervisele tekitatud püsikahjud'. In *Valge raamat: eesti rahva kaotustest okupatsioonide läbi 1940–1991*, edited by Ülo Ennuste, Erast Parmasto, Enn Tarvel, and Peep Varju, 53–66. Tallinn: Justiitsministeerium, 2005.

Paavle, Indrek. 'Kes ei tööta, ei pea ka sööma'. In *Tuna* 3 (2015): 75–89.

Pagel, Oliver. 'Soome turistid Eesti NSVs aastail 1955–1980'. In *Eesti Ajalooarhiivi toimetised* 23/30, edited by Tõnu Tannberg, 279–98. Tartu: Eesti Ajalooarhiiv 2015.

Pall, Ilmar. 'Kuuekümnendad. Kummalised, mitte kuldsed. Intervjuu Teet Kallasega', *KesKus*, 2 August 2004, http://kes -kus.ee/kuuekumnendad-kummalised-mitte-kuldsed-kirjanik

-teet-kallas-raagib-ilmar-pallile-oma-kuuekumnendaist-mis
-temale-ei-saranud-hoopiski-nii-kuldselt-kui-monele-tema
-kolleegile/. Accessed 16 July 2021.

Palu, Johannes. 'Tuumatalv'. In *Harju Elu* 14 (29 January 1985): 2–3.

Pilkington, Hilary. 'Punk, but Not as we Know it: Rethinking
Punk from a Post-socialist Perspective'. In *Punk in Russia:
Cultural Mutation from the 'Useless' to the 'Moronic'*, edited by
Ivan Gololobov, Hilary Pilkington, and Yngvar B. Steinholt,
1–21. London: Routledge, 2014.

Piotrowska, Anna G. 'European Pop Music and the Notion of
Protest'. In *The Routledge History of Social Protest in Popular
Music*ed, edited by Jonathan C. Friedman. Abingdon:
Routledge Handbooks Online, 2013.

Põlluste, Grete. *ENSV Tööliste Internatsionaalse Liikumise juhtkonna
sotsiaalne kooslus*. Tartu: Tartu Ülikool, 2019.

Rahi-Tamm, Aigi. 'Inimkaotused'. In *Valge raamat: eesti rahva
kaotustest okupatsioonide läbi 1940–1991*, edited by Ülo
Ennuste, Erast Parmasto, Enn Tarvel, and Peep Varju, 23–42.
Tallinn: Justiitsministeerium, 2005.

Reynolds, Simon. *Retromania*. New York: Faber and Faber, 2011.

Rinne, Harri. *Laulev revolutsioon. Eesti rokipõlvkonna ime*. Tallinn:
Varrak, 2008.

Salumets, Vello. *Rockrapsoodia*. Tallinn: Eesti
Entsüklopeediakirjastus, 1998.

Sarv, Enn and Peep Varju. 'Ülevaade okupatsioonidest'. In *Valge
raamat: eesti rahva kaotustest okupatsioonide läbi 1940–1991*,
edited by Ülo Ennuste, Erast Parmasto, Enn Tarvel, and Peep
Varju, 9–22. Tallinn: Justiitsministeerium, 2005.

Savisaar, Edgar. 'Edgar Savisaare appikutse Toompealt –
Toompead rünnatakse!'. In *ERR*, 15 May 1990. https://arhiiv
.err.ee/audio/vaata/edgar-savisaare-appikutse-toompealt
-toompead-runnatakse. Accessed 29 August 2023.

Šmidchens, Guntis. *The Power of Song: Nonviolent National Culture in the Baltic Singing Revolution*. Seattle: University of Washington Press, 2014.

Suurkas, Heiki. 'Nelja aastaga iseseisvaks: 1988 – konflikt Tartus, isamaalised laulud, ERSP ja Rahvarinne'. *Eesti Päevaleht*, 13 August 2016.

Swift, John. 'The Soviet-American Arms Race'. In *History Today*, March 2009. https://www.historytoday.com/archive/soviet -american-arms-race. Accessed 10 August 2023.

Tamme, Villu. 'Tobe raamat'. *Looming* 3 (2001): 463–6.

Tammela, Hiljar. 'Parteiline Poliitilise Informatsiooni töötlemise süsteem Eesti NSV-s 1944–1940'. In *Propaganda, sisseränne ja monumendid, Eesti Mälu Instituudi toimetised*, 11–47. Tartu ja Tallinn: Tartu Ülikooli ja Eesti Mälu Instituut, 2021.

Tammela, Hiljar. 'Sissejuhatus'. In *Propaganda, sisseränne ja monumendid. Eesti Mälu Instituudi toimetised*, 7–9. Tartu ja Tallinn: Tartu Ülikooli Kirjastus ja Eesti Mälu Instituut, 2021.

Tannberg, Tõnu. '"Lubjanka marssal" Nõukogude impeeriumi äärealasid reformimas. L. Beria rahvuspoliitika eesmärkidest ja tagajärgedest 1953. aastal III'. In *Tuna* 1 (2000): 42–52.

Tannberg, Tõnu. '1953. aasta amnestia: kas ainult varaste ja sulide vabastamine?'. In *Tuna* 3 (2004): 37–51.

Tannberg, Tõnu. 'Taasiseseisvumine'. In *Eesti ajalugu VI*, 374–90. Tartu: Ilmamaa, 2005.

Tannberg, Tõnu. 'Gorbatšov ei toonud meile vabadust'. *ERR*, 31 August 2022.

Tooming, Peeter. 'Valitsus V'. In *Ringvaade 'Nõukogude Eesti'*, 1987, 20. Accessed 19 July 2023.

Toomistu, Terje. 'Such a Strange Vibration: Rock Music as the Affective Site of Divergence among the Soviet Estonian Nonconformist Youth'. In *Res Musica* 10 (2018): 11–27.

Traube, Elisabeth. 'Introduction'. In *Making and Selling Culture*, edited by Richard Ohmann. xi–xxiii. Hanover: Wesleyan University Press, 1996.

Turk, Pirjo. 'Eesti punk – miilitsast presidendini'. In *Subkultuurid: Elustiilide uurimused*, edited by Airi-Alina Allaste, 79–118. Tallinn: TLÜ Kirjastus, 2013.

Vainola, Allan. *Inventuur*. Tallinn: Menu kirjastus OÜ, 2011.

Vaksberg, Arkadi. '1941. aasta oktoobri saladus'. *Pärnu Kommunist* 81, 28 April 1988, 3.

Värv, Ellen. 'Noored 1950.–1960. aastate Eesti NSV-s'. In *Eesti Rahva Muuseumi aastaraamat* 49, 11–48. Tartu: Eesti Rahva Muuseum, 2006.

Veiderma, Mihkel. *Tagasivaade eluteele*. Tallinn: Eesti Keele Sihtasutus, 2009.

Ventsel, Aimar. 'Materdatud kaltsakatest perestroika-aja kangelasteks'. *Sirp*, 16 March 2018, 10–12.

Viires, Piret. 'Eesti punkluule ja siirdeajastu algus'. In *Philologia Estonica Tallinnensis* 6 (2021): 36–52.

Interviews

Hardi Volmer. Interview, 8 February 2021.

Joose Berglund. Interview, 1 September 2022.

Lembit Krull. Facebook chat 2022–2023.

Rein Lang. Interview, 14 December 2020.

Villu Tamme. Interview, 20 July 2022.

Index